The Children Act Report
1995 – 1999

A report by the Secretary of State for Health, the Secretary of State for Education and Employment and the Lord Chancellor on the Children Act 1989 in pursuance of their duties under section 83(6) of the Act, presented to Parliament by Command of Her Majesty: January 2000.

Cm 4579

£15.70

Executive Summary

The main purposes of the report are set out in the Introduction. These are to provide information to Parliament on the Act as is required statutorily; to describe the main changes and developments since the last report (1995); and, to set a new framework to track progress on a number of initiatives, principally the Quality Protects(QP) programme. The report covers England.

Chapter 1 sets the context for children's services. It highlights some of the legal amendments to the Children Act since 1994 and to reports, such as the *Safeguards Review (1997)*, which have resulted in the Government's concerted drive to tackle child protection and reform services for looked after children through the Quality Protects programme. In this context, the 8 original QP objectives are listed and their relationship to the Children Act explained. There is discussion about ethnic monitoring and its introduction next year into routine DH collection for children's services. The importance of children's participation within the Act and QP is highlighted.

Part 2 of the report comprises Chapters 2-9. These discuss respectively the 8 Quality Protects objectives, each of which is summarised as the chapter heading and set out in full as the sub-heading.

Chapter 2 'Secure attachment and stability' provides an overview of the Government's programme to secure the well-being of children and supporting partnerships *(Supporting Families 1998)*. These include the National Family and Parenting Institute, the Sure Start programme and early years initiatives. SSI findings on family support are covered, followed by detailed text and tables about children looked after, including short-term placements and stability of care within local authorities. Full details about adoption, including patterns of adoption from care and SSI findings on adoption and post adoption services are included.

Chapter 3 'Child protection' provides an account of the patterns of child abuse and child protection register numbers, registrations and de-registrations. This is followed by the key messages in the new consultative draft *Working Together (1999;* relevant SSI inspection findings; data on re- registration patterns; and whether cases are allocated to a social worker. The chapter discusses the increased use of care and supervision orders in order to secure the health and development of children.

Chapter 4 'Life chances of children in need' begins with a discussion about the definition of 'children in need' and then highlights four areas concerning the welfare of children with a social exclusion perspective. These are young carers, school inclusion, child and adolescent mental health and youth offending. There follows a discussion about the measurement of life chances and possible future approaches to measuring outcomes for children in need but not looked after with a summary of available data for all children regarding education, health and offending.

Chapter 5 'Life chances of looked after children' identifies educational attainment as the single most important indicator of children's life chances and summarises both OFSTED and SEU reports about looked after children (1995) and truancy and school exclusion (1998). Outcome measures other than educational attainment are summarised and are followed by details of new national statistical collections which have been introduced to monitor outcome and performance indicators for looked after children.

Chapter 6 'Life chances for care leavers' concerns children who at the age of about 16 are being looked after and are entering adulthood heavily dependant on local authority support. Their future is known to be precarious and the QP objective is about the provision of support at a critical stage of transition. The chapter also includes data on numbers and circumstances of care leavers; reference to the recent consultation paper (*Me, Survive, Out There?*); support for care-leavers; and messages from SSI inspections.

Chapter 7 'Services for disabled children and their families' recognises that information about disabled children is outdated; then summarises from various sources what is known and sets out the case for improved information. The chapter also covers the relevance of several of the QP objectives to this group of children; SSI inspection messages; and opportunities for multi-agency service co-ordination with emphasis on the user perspective.

Chapter 8 'Assessment and decision making' stresses from research and inspection findings the importance of assessments and details the recently issued DH consultative draft (*Framework for the Assessment of Children in Need and their Families*). It emphasises the use of evidence when making judgements about children's welfare and whether and how best to provide services for children and families.

Chapter 9 'Resource planning' responds to a specific request from the Select Committee for detailed information on resources and costs. Some of the factors that explain how local authorities respond to need and the variations between them are explored including patterns of expenditure on looked after children and different kinds of care; the supply side, such as approved foster carers and available residential care; the underlying needs and demand.

This chapter also discusses progress on information about how resources for children's personal social services are used; Departmental information on expenditure on children in need; children's services planning and relevant SSI inspection findings.

Part 3 of the report mainly concerns areas of the Children Act where the Lord Chancellor's Department and the Department for Education and Employment have the policy lead.

Chapter 10 ' Activity in the Courts' summarises the range of orders available in 'family proceedings' and in addition to the Children Act, the range of statutes whose provisions also are treated as family proceedings. Trends in both private and public law orders under the Act are described. This chapter also summaries the work of the guardian ad litem and reporting officer service; the review of court welfare services (1998); and the Government's decision (1999) to establish a unified service when legislative time permits. The private law Children Act activity does not fall within Quality Protects. Other policy developments mentioned are The Children Act Advisory Committee; the Advisory Board on Family Law and care planning.

Chapter 11 'Early Years' provides information about the National Childcare Strategy (1998). There follow data about day nurseries, childminders, day-care places and out of school and holiday schemes.

The report's four annexes list relevant SSI inspection reports and other key references. Current or recently completed research on aspects of family support and support to parenting are also included. All amendments to the Children Act and regulations under the Act since 1994 are set out.

Table of Contents
Preface
Introduction

PART I THE CONTEXT FOR CHILDREN'S SERVICES TODAY

Chapter I The Context for Children's Services Today   *2*

PART 2 NATIONAL OBJECTIVES FOR THE CHILDREN'S SOCIAL SERVICES

Chapter 2 Secure Attachment and Stability   *10*

Chapter 3 Child Protection   *32*

Chapter 4 Life Chances of Children in Need   *42*

Tables

Figures

Annexes

Preface

This report provides information on the impact of the Children Act 1989. It describes the main changes and developments in recent years and sets these within the new policy framework of the Government's objectives for children's social services and the Quality Protects programme. The report reflects our growing understanding of the working of the Act derived from a wide range of sources. These include research, statistics, inspections, reviews and inquiries including the report of the Health Select Committee on Children Looked After which called for the resumed publication of annual Children Act Reports.

The Children Act came into effect in October 1991. It provides the framework for the delivery of services and court-related proceedings concerning a wide range of children. We have set clear objectives for children's services. These objectives express many of the intentions of the Children Act. Achieving them is the responsibility of all concerned – central and local government, the health service and the voluntary sector. Future Children Act reports will track the progress made in taking forward these objectives and the Quality Protects programme.

Alan Milburn
Secretary of State for Health

December 1999

Introduction

This report fulfils three main purposes by:

• providing the information to Parliament required by Section 83 of the Children Act

• describing the main changes and developments since the last Children Act Report was published in 1995 and

• setting the framework for a series of reports which will track progress on a number of initiatives – notably the Quality Protects programme – aimed at improving the delivery of services to children, improving their protection and advancing their health and welfare.

It sets changes since the last report in the wider context of a deeper understanding of the working of the Act – as a result of research, statistics, inspections, reviews and inquiries – and summarises the main policy developments and initiatives which have resulted from this.

It takes as the framework for the body of the report the Government's objectives for children's services, announced with the Quality Protects initiative. It describes the current state of knowledge on those areas and the action being taken. Subsequent reports in this series will track progress in meeting the Quality Protects Objectives and report on further action.

The report is presented in three parts with annexes. Part 1 provides a concise overview of the current policy context for children's personal social services. Part 2 looks at eight objectives for children's services and sets out the evidence of current performance against these objectives. Part 3 covers areas of the Act which mainly fall within the remit of the Lord Chancellor's Department and the Department for Education and Employment.

PART 1
The Context for Children's Services Today

The Context for Children's Services Today

Developments since 1994-95

1.1 There have been a number of amendments to the Children Act since 1994 and to regulations made under the Act. These are set out in full at Annex D.

1.2 Some of the most important changes are:

   – new powers to add exclusion requirements to interim care orders and emergency protection orders where domestic violence is an issue, allowing the child to remain at home but the violent person to be removed

   – providing for certain orders under the Crime and Disorder Act 1998 to be made in family proceedings

   – linking the Family Law Act 1996 with the Children Act by designating FLA applications as 'family proceedings' (see Chapter 10)

   – extending the range of children who can qualify for advice and assistance to those who are accommodated in health authority settings

   – to regulations restricting the opportunities for those with criminal records for offences against children to be employed or considered for fostering, adoption or work in certain settings with children

   – to require Local Authorities to prepare plans for the provision of children's services in their area and to keep those plans under review.

1.3 There have also been several developments which have had a significant impact on how the expectations of the Children Act are delivered.

Measures to protect children from abuse and poor care

1.4 These changes have been made against a background of continuing concern about the effectiveness of child care protection arrangements as shown in a number of inquiry reports and other important documents:

   · Childhood Matters: The Report of the National Commission of Inquiry into the Prevention of Child Abuse. (1996).

   · People Like us: The Report of the Review of the Safeguards for Children Living Away from Home. (1997)

   · Children Looked After by Local Authorities: Second Report of the Health Committee (1998).

1.5   As a result of these concerns, the Government has launched over the last year a concerted drive to tackle the issue through a series of initiatives including:

- Quality Protects

- the new National Priorities Guidance for health and social services

- the Response to the Children's Safeguards Review

- the Social Services White Paper - *Modernising Social Services*

- *Children Looked After by Local Authorities:* the Government's response to the Health Committee Report.

Children's Services Planning

1.6   An order made under the Children Act 1989, which came into force on 1 April 1996, required local authorities to plan children's services. This necessitated a review of services for children in need and consultation with other agencies in order to make plans for how these services would develop.

1.7   Subsequent studies of the planning process by the Social Services Inspectorate (*Partners in Planning* (1998)) and National Children's Bureau (*Children's Services Plans Analysing Need: Reallocating Resources* (1998)) found that:

- local authorities were beginning to consider how the whole authority could improve the lot of children by lifting discussion above traditional agency boundaries. It was found that involving other agencies was difficult

- users were seldom involved in the planning process and ethnic minority groups were under-recognised

- changing the type or range of services provided was a slow process.

1.8   The rapid development of a wide range of planning requirements, the recognition of the need for more coherence, as a result of the work of the Social Exclusion Unit, and the clear requirement for better management information in response to the Health Select Committee's *Second Report on Children Looked After by Local Authorities* have led to:

- a commitment to strengthen the planning process so as to increase its corporate and interagency effectiveness and

- a drive to improve the use of management information through the Quality Protects programme.

Framework for the Report

1.9   Quality Protects sets clear objectives for those providing children's services. Most of the remainder of this report focuses on those objectives. It explains:

- the outcomes which the objectives are designed to achieve

- the information available to assess how far they are being achieved

- what action is underway and what may be needed in future.

1.10   It draws on information obtained from the inspection work of the Social Services Inspectorate (SSI). Annex A provides a synopsis of research work that has recently been completed or is currently underway.

1.11   In a number of cases the available statistical information is not well geared to the new need to monitor these objectives. Future action will involve making changes to the information collected in order to do so. This report sets the baseline against which progress will be measured and an agenda for action to ensure that monitoring is both possible and effective. The report covers England only.

1.12   The report also includes chapters on court activity and services for children in their early years.

1.13   An up-date of this report containing further statistics for 1999 that are not yet available will be provided later. Annual reports will then be produced from Autumn 2000 onwards.

How the objectives relate to the Children Act

1.14   The Children Act requires that those responsible for the upbringing of children should *safeguard and promote their welfare*. This term is used in:

- Section 3 which sets out the meaning of parental responsibility

- Section 17 which sets out local authorities' duty to provide a range of services for children in need, their families and others

- Section 22 which sets out the duties of local authorities in relation to children they look after.

In court proceedings, Section 1 emphasises the paramount welfare of the child.

1.15   The Act says little else about objectives. By far the greater part of the Act is concerned with the practices and procedures when courts and local authorities intervene in the lives of children and their families with a view to safeguarding and promoting children's welfare.

1.16   The Act does not define 'welfare' but it does provide a useful guide to its meaning in the way it defines a 'child in need'. Section 17(10) says that a child is in need if, without the provision of services, he:

- is unlikely to achieve or maintain a reasonable standard of health and development or

- his health and development is likely to be impaired, or

- he is disabled.

1.17 Eight comprehensive and outcome-focused objectives for the personal social services for children were published with the launch of the Quality Protects Programme in September and in November 1998, in slightly amended form, along with objectives for adults, in the Social Services White Paper *Modernising Social Services.*

1.18 The eight objectives were:

- **to ensure that children are securely attached to carers capable of providing safe and effective care for the duration of childhood**

- **to ensure that children are protected from emotional, physical, sexual abuse and neglect (significant harm)**

- **to ensure that children gain maximum life chance benefits from educational opportunities, health care and social care**

- **to ensure that children looked after gain maximum life chance benefits from educational opportunities, health care and social care**

- **to ensure that young people leaving care, as they enter adulthood, are not isolated and participate socially and economical as citizens**

- **to ensure that children with specific social needs arising out of disability or a health condition are living in families or other appropriate settings in the community where their assessed needs are adequately met and reviewed**

- **to ensure that referral and assessment processes discriminate effectively between different types and levels of need and produce a timely service response**

- **to ensure that resources are planned and provided at levels which represent best value for money, allow for choice and different responses for different needs and circumstances.**

Chapters 2 to 9 address each of the above objectives.

1.19 The first objective is concerned with securing the primary conditions for the health and development of children – a secure and stable attachment to parents or carers whom they can trust to go on caring for them.

1.20 The need to safeguard children and to protect them from significant harm is expressed in the second objective.

1.21 The promotion of children's welfare is covered by the next three objectives which seek better life chances for looked after children and those leaving care.

1.22 The sixth objective concerns services for children with disabilities. This objective is derived almost directly from the responsibilities set out in part III of the Children Act 1989.

1.23 The remaining two objectives concern assessment, decision making and service response and work in reference to listening to children and planning for the most effective and best value range of services. The former, particularly as augmented with the sub-objectives, brings a performance standard to assessment and the provision of services in terms of speed of response.

1.24   The objectives make explicit what is implicit in the Children Act. In effect, they expand on the meaning of safeguarding and promoting children's welfare and they strengthen some of the strategic planning underpinning of the Act which has been put in place since its implementation. They are not intended to fetter the discretion of the judiciary in making decisions under the Children Act.

1.25   At the same time as the launch of Quality Protects, the Department of Health sought views on the associated sub-objectives and performance indicators. Taking account of the views of those consulted, the Department is publishing a full set of children's Quality Protects performance indicators. These have been expanded to eleven objectives by incorporating those held in common with adult services. Many of those indicators will form part of the Performance Assessment Framework for social services and some will be Best Value Indicators. Local authorities' performance in achieving the objectives and sub-objectives will be monitored through annual Quality Protects Management Action Plans, reports and through the Social Services Inspectorate's regular assessment of authorities' progress against the Performance Assessment Framework. Annual Children Act reports will reflect that monitoring and progress.

Ethnicity

1.26   The objectives for children's personal social services apply to all children irrespective of their racial, cultural, religious or linguistic identity. But information from research and inspection indicates that these factors show up significant differences in children's access to services. For example, children with dual black and white parentage are over-represented among looked after children, and Asian children tend to be under-represented. When controlled for age and duration of the care episode, the figures reveal more complex patterns.

1.27   Ethnic monitoring will be introduced into routine statistical collections on children's services from the year 2000. Until then, it is not possible to provide information about how children from minority ethnic groups fare with respect to the objectives. The Department of Health is committed to introducing collections of statistical information on ethnicity. It will be included in existing and proposed collections, in particular, the collection on looked after children and the new collection of expenditure on children in need, and will be based on the sixteen codes for ethnicity proposed for the 2001 Census. This will mean that, during the course of 2000-2001, it will be possible to provide information on:

•   how ethnicity is related to the reasons for children needing help from social services

•   the actual services children from ethnic minorities receive and

•   the associated expenditure.

1.28   It will also be possible to provide breakdowns by ethnicity of the detailed statistical information on looked after children.

1.29   Although the objectives relate to all children, the way services are targeted and applied must vary in relation to how particular ethnic groups are fully embraced. How this is achieved will be different for different ethnic communities. Specialised services will need to be planned on the basis of certain information. Some local authorities, for example, already record detailed information about race, language, religion and culture. By introducing ethnicity into national collections, the Department will be requiring all local authorities to collect data which is also needed for their own management and planning purposes. The results of these statistical returns will inform future Children Act reports.

Children's participation

1.30   Promoting children's participation is an important theme underpinning the Children Act and given further emphasis in Quality Protects. Its importance arises because children have too often been marginalised, or completely excluded, where key decisions are being made about their future. Children's ability to offer constructive comment on their experiences of the services they receive and how such services might be improved has been under-valued and under-used.

1.31   Listening to the views and wishes of children and young people is one of the current priorities under the children's services special grant announced in November 1998 and underpinning Quality Protects. The aim is to help local authorities significantly increase children's participation in the development of local authority services and to allow children's views to inform local planning and national policy making.

1.32   Local authorities need to demonstrate that children's views are reflected in planning, monitoring and evaluating children's services and further to develop monitoring of user satisfaction, as measured by surveys, inspection and other performance indicators. Authorities need also to involve particular groups of children such as young carers.

1.33   Subsequent Children Act reports will comment in more depth on local authorities' performance in promoting children's participation.

PART 2
National Objectives for Children's Social Services

Secure Attachment and Stability

Objective: To ensure that children are securely attached to carers capable of providing safe and effective care for the duration of childhood.

Introduction

2.1 If they are to grow into dependable adults, fully capable of forming loving relationships, children must be looked after by parents or carers whom they can trust, and whose care is consistent, warm and positive. Transience undermines children's ability to learn. Interventions under the Children Act, whether by the provision of family support, by acting to protect children and/or decisions in courts, have to set the conditions which offer the best chance for children to experience secure and stable attachments.

2.2 To assess how effective the personal social services are at achieving this objective, it is necessary to look at what happens to children who:

- stay in their own families

- are at the boundary between family care and local authority care or

- are looked after by the local authority.

2.3 The amount of information available for each of these circumstances varies considerably.

Stability and turmoil in families

2.4 Out of 11 million children and young people under 18 years old in England:

- some 8.5 million live in two parent families

- 2.5 million in single parent families and;

- about 350,000 are estimated to be in contact with social services at any one time

- 50,000 are looked after by local authorities.

2.5 The Government has embarked on a programme designed to help secure the well-being of children and protect partnerships. The details of this family policy were set out in the consultation document *"Supporting Families"* issued in November 1998. The five key themes have a strong focus on the needs of children and recognise that children are best served through direct help to families. These themes are to:

- ensure all families have access to the advice and support they need

- improve family prosperity and reduce poverty through the tax and benefit system

- make it easier for families to balance work and home

- strengthen marriage and reduce the risks of family breakdown

- tackle the more serious problems of family life - such as domestic violence, truancy and school-age pregnancy.

2.6   The policy recognises the importance of good parenting. A National Family and Parenting Institute is being set up to provide authoritative evidence-based advice to the Government and others on such issues. A new national parenting helpline is also being made available to offer parents confidential advice. The helpline is intended to act as a gateway to a range of other services for parents and families. The Social Exclusion Unit has an important role – poverty and racial discrimination contribute significantly to social exclusion.

2.7   The Sure Start programme will also provide a focus for better parenting help and information. Sure Start is a cross-cutting programme designed to promote the physical, social, emotional and intellectual development of children from birth to the age of four. It aims to have some 250 local programmes running, in the areas of greatest need, by the end of this Parliament. Parenting advice and support is a core service within these programmes.

2.8   In the area of Early Years provision, local Early Excellence Centres for young children and their families will also provide such support. These centres are also a part of the move towards increased co-ordination and joint planning through the introduction of the Early Years Development and Childcare Partnerships.

2.9   Schools also have an important role in ensuring the next generation of children is better prepared for the responsibilities of parenthood. They are being encouraged to work further on a partnership approach with parents to help develop skills in effective communication with young people, particularly on such issues as parenthood, relationships and sex. The arrangements for sex education, for example, require that teaching be provided in a manner which encourages pupils to have proper regard to the value of family life.

2.10   The contribution of local authority social services is to support families by providing a range of services for them and children in need.

2.11   In March 1999, the Social Services Inspectorate published its report *"Getting Family Support Right".* The report presented the findings of an inspection in the delivery of family support services within eight authorities. Community social work, child and adolescent mental health (CAMH) social work, and family centres were the three main issues that were looked at within family support services, and information from 2,323 families (studying 80 cases in detail) was collected as part of this inspection.

2.12   Some of the key findings from a substantial number of cases showed possible indicators where abuse or neglect of children had not been properly recognised or assessed. A need was also seen for greater understanding of the impact of emotional abuse on children and the appropriate intervention mechanisms that needed to be put in place.

2.13   The inspection found that family centres offered an increasingly wide range of innovative services. They made extremely good use of scarce resources, and parents particularly valued outreach work, parenting skills training and support groups. Social workers were providing a number of creative packages for children. While 25% of children had parents with mental health needs, relationships between childcare and adult health social workers were found to be ineffective and often poor.

2.14   Child and adolescent mental health social workers provided a range of valuable and effective services in conjunction with their health and education colleagues. However, they were better at working jointly within their own settings than with colleagues from outside. Also found was conflict between the managers of the employing agencies in six of the authorities.

2.15   Only one authority was implementing a clear strategy for delivering family support services. Most authorities had not developed clear priorities for allocating resources or determining who was eligible for services. Many managers, for example, found it hard to hold on to their own priorities as well as to the many new joint planning requirements being driven by other agency initiatives. Authorities were only at the very beginning of developing a comprehensive approach to monitoring services and evaluating their effectiveness.

2.16   Although the report sets out the outcome of delivery of family support services, it also provides guidance for managers of family support services so as to ensure that families are offered appropriate and effective support, and that children at risk of significant harm are identified and protected. It has done this by identifying the methods that were most effective in achieving appropriate outcomes for children and their families. In addition to the main report, a Summary report was also issued to practitioners and first-line managers, highlighting good practice and providing suggestions to improve their work with children and families.

2.17   In Resource Planning (Chapter 9), information is given about how expenditure on children's services nationally is divided between providing family support services and providing for children looked after by local authorities. There is evidence that over a number of years the proportion of spend on family support has been increasing although the increase in the numbers of children looked after over the last four or five years may curtail this trend. The ratio of spend between family support and children looked after is a measure of the extent to which family support is being prioritised and this is now included as a performance indicator within Quality Protects and the Performance Assessment Framework.

The interface of family and local authority care

Recent trends in figures for looked after children

2.18 Figures illustrating the size and composition of the population of looked after children in England are given in Table 2.1.

Table 2.1 Children looked after at 31 March by age, sex, placement and legal status 1992-1998

England — numbers, percentages and rates per 10,000 children under 18

	numbers							percentages						
	1992	1993	1994	1995	1996	1997	1998	1992	1993	1994	1995	1996	1997	1998
All children[1]	**55,500**	**51,600**	**49,300**	**49,800**	**50,600**	**51,400**	**53,300**	*100*	*100*	*100*	*100*	*100*	*100*	*100*
rate per 10,000 children	51	47	45	45	45	46	47							
Sex														
Boys	29,300	27,300	26,300	26,600	27,400	28,100	29,100	*53*	*53*	*53*	*53*	*54*	*55*	*55*
Girls	26,100	24,300	23,000	23,100	23,200	23,400	24,200	*47*	*47*	*47*	*46*	*46*	*45*	*45*
Age														
Under 1	1,420	1,310	1,450	1,590	1,630	1,710	1,750	*3*	*3*	*3*	*3*	*3*	*3*	*3*
1 -4	8,100	6,800	6,500	6,800	7,300	8,200	8,700	*15*	*13*	*13*	*14*	*14*	*16*	*16*
5 - 9	11,900	10,900	10,300	10,200	10,500	10,900	11,700	*21*	*21*	*21*	*20*	*21*	*21*	*22*
10 - 15	21,900	21,400	21,300	21,800	21,600	21,500	21,700	*39*	*41*	*43*	*44*	*43*	*42*	*41*
16 and over	12,200	11,200	9,900	9,500	9,500	9,100	9,400	*22*	*22*	*20*	*19*	*19*	*18*	*18*
Placement														
Foster placements	32,400	31,400	31,300	32,100	33,000	33,500	35,100	*58*	*61*	*63*	*64*	*65*	*65*	*66*
Children's homes	9,000	8,100	7,400	7,200	6,700	6,500	6,500	*16*	*16*	*15*	*14*	*13*	*13*	*12*
Placed with parents	6,400	5,100	4,500	4,400	4,700	5,200	5,600	*12*	*10*	*9*	*9*	*9*	*10*	*11*
Placed for adoption	2,800	2,500	2,200	2,200	2,200	2,400	2,500	*5*	*5*	*4*	*4*	*4*	*5*	*5*
In lodgings, residential employment or living independently	2,100	2,000	1,500	1,400	1,400	1,200	1,200	*4*	*4*	*3*	*3*	*3*	*2*	*2*
Other placement	2,800	2,500	2,400	2,500	2,500	2,500	2,700	*5*	*5*	*5*	*5*	*5*	*5*	*5*
Legal Status														
Care Orders	37,500	31,800	29,100	28,700	28,900	30,100	31,900	*68*	*62*	*59*	*58*	*57*	*58*	*60*
S20 CA 1989 (voluntary agreements)	17,100	18,500	18,800	19,500	19,900	19,400	19,200	*31*	*36*	*38*	*39*	*39*	*38*	*36*
On remand, committed for trial or detained	390	430	420	430	480	490	610	*1*	*1*	*1*	*1*	*1*	*1*	*1*
Other legal status	490	930	990	1,100	1,200	1,400	1,700	*1*	*2*	*2*	*2*	*2*	*3*	*3*

1 Figures for children looked after in this table exclude agreed series of short term placements

Figure 2.1 Number of children looked after, the number in foster placements and residential placements at 31 March 1988 to 1998

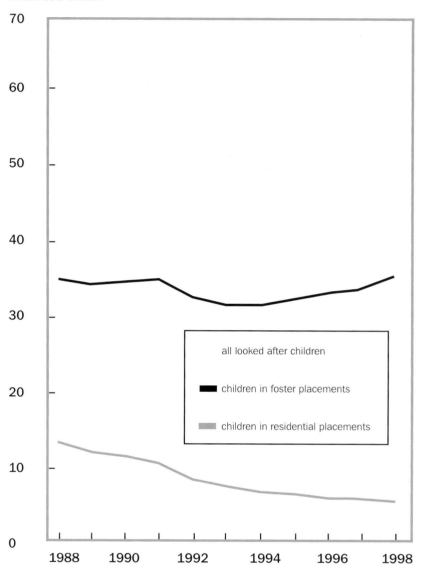

thousands of children

2.19   The longstanding downward trend in overall numbers of looked after children, long pre-dating the implementation of the Children Act, and reflecting the policy that children were, in most cases, better off living with their own families than elsewhere, ended in 1994 (Table 2.1). There had been a particularly marked decline in the use of residential care. The numbers of children in foster placements fell less sharply and the proportion of children looked after in foster care increased.

2.20   Between 1994 and 1998 there was an 8% rise in the numbers of children looked after (see Figure 2.1). Over this period there were increases in the number of children:

- in foster placements

- placed for adoption

- and on care orders placed with parents.

2.21 In contrast, the number of children in residential care and in lodgings continued to decline. Two thirds of looked after children are now cared for in foster placements, compared with 58% in 1992.

2.22 More boys are looked after than girls, and the proportion of boys has risen in recent years (Table 2.1). The number and proportion of younger children looked after is also increasing. At 31 March 1998, 20% of all looked after children were under 5 years old, compared with 16% in 1994.

2.23 The use of care orders is increasing. 60% of looked after children at 31 March 1998 were looked after under care orders, 1,800 more than a year earlier. In contrast, the proportion of looked after children under voluntary agreements (Section 20 Children Act 1989) has fallen recently.

Children beginning and ceasing to be looked after by local authorities

2.24 During 1997/98, 26 children out of every 10,000 aged under 18 started to be looked after. There is considerable variation between local authorities, with rates varying from 7 per 10,000 children to over 70.

2.25 This variation is explained by a mixture of underlying pressure to respond to children's social care needs, local policies and other local factors. Chapter 8 discusses how far applying an index of underlying need can help to explain variations between authorities. In the case of children entering local authority care, underlying need explains only about 20% of this variation. This suggests that local policies may play a much more significant part in determining how many children become looked after.

Table 2.2 Children starting to be looked after during 1996/97 by numbers of starts during 1996/97 and reason for being looked after for their last start

England   numbers and percentages

	numbers				percentages			
	All children	Children who had 2 or more starts in 1996/97	Children who had 5 or more starts in 1996/97	Children who had 10 or more starts in 1996/97	All children	Children who had 2 or more starts in 1996/97	Children who had 5 or more starts in 1996/97	Children who had 10 or more starts in 1996/97
All children[1]	**29,900**	**4,900**	**390**	**90**	*100*	*100*	*100*	*100*
Reason for being looked after								
Parents need relief	7,800	1,800	250	70	*26*	*37*	*64*	*78*
Abuse or neglect	7,000	600	10	-	*23*	*12*	*2*	-
Parent's health	3,600	670	40	10	*12*	*14*	*10*	*11*
Child's welfare	2,500	360	10	-	*8*	*7*	*2*	-
Offence	1,500	330	20	-	*5*	*7*	*5*	-
Own behaviour	1,500	320	10	-	*5*	*7*	*3*	-
Request of child	900	110	-	-	*3*	*2*	-	-
Abandoned or lost	880	80	5	-	*3*	*2*	*1*	-
Other	4,300	540	50	10	*14*	*11*	*13*	*12*

1 Excludes agreed series of short term placements

2.26   Table 2.2 shows the number of children who experienced repeated admissions to local authority care during the course of a year. It excludes all cases reported to the Department as having agreements for a planned series of short term (respite) placements. During 1996-97:

- about one in six children admitted to local authority care during the course of a year were admitted more than once,

- some 390 children had 5 or more admissions during the course of a year.

2.27   Although these numbers are small, if they represent unplanned responses to chronic problems of family care, they are likely to have caused a good deal of distress to the children which might have been alleviated by careful assessment and planning. If, at least in part, they represent situations in which children have benefited from a planned series of short term placements with the same carers on each occasion, then local authorities may wish to review how they record these cases in statistical returns.

Figure 2.2 Proportion of children who started to be looked after during 1996/97 who had had a previous care history, by local authority

number of local authorities

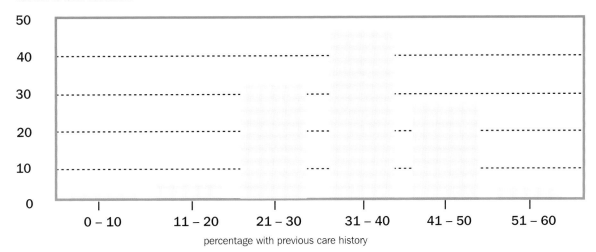

percentage with previous care history

2.28 Figure 2.2 shows the wide spread between authorities of the proportion of looked after children who have had previous periods of local authority care. From this can be derived the proportion of looked after children who have never been looked after before. It is clearly very common for between 30% and 40% of children to have had previous care experiences, but in one authority this is as high as 53% and in another as low as 8%. This suggests very different patterns in the use of public care to support children and families. Local authorities at the extremes, particularly those with rates above 40%, may wish to examine why their procedures or practices result in these levels of repeated care experiences for children.

2.29 The general point is whether becoming looked after is:

- a planned event aimed, in the long term, at supporting children in their families,

- a passage into a new phase of life which is geared to securing stability in another care setting, or

- a haphazard unplanned episode in children's lives which adds to their instability and turmoil.

The published statistics for children looked after enable each authority to assess their performance against all other authorities. As is the intention behind the Performance Assessment Framework, by seeking to explain why they occupy a given position, authorities will discover more about their practices and the scope for making their services more effective.

Messages from Inspection

Someone Else's Children: The Inspections of Planning and Decision - Making for Children Looked After and The Inspection of Safety of Children Looked After (1998) found:

- commitment to working in partnership with parents was strong but sometimes led to excessive attempts to rehabilitate children home

- little indication of children coming into public care who did not need to

- placements were too often crisis driven and there was a lack of placement choices, particularly for those with special needs

- individual needs of children were compromised by the tendency to focus short term objectives in care plans

- a problem of finding placements to reflect the racial, cultural and linguistic background of ethnic minority children.

The contribution of planned series of short-term placements

2.30   Table 2.3 shows an overall increase in the use of a planned series of short-term placements from 9,400 children in 1994 to 11,000 in 1998, although this rise may reflect improvements in the reporting of these children over this period. There is enormous variation between local authorities. Some of this variation may be the result of:

- different interpretations of the legal provision and the administrative categories used in recording;

- different practices in the recording of support for families caring for disabled children. Some authorities treat such children as not looked after at all, so that they do not appear in these or other statistics.

2.31   These variations are thought to affect the figures presented here but it is believed that recording and reporting practices are becoming more consistent.

2.32   Planned short term care has been traditionally thought of as a means of supporting families caring for disabled children but families caring for children with difficulties other than disability might also be supported by this provision. Table 2.3 shows that about half the children receiving a series of short term placements are recorded as looked after for reasons other than disability.

Table 2.3 Children looked after during the year under at least one series of short term placements, years ending 31 March 1994 to 1998

England   numbers and percentages

	numbers					percentages				
	1994	1995	1996	1997	1998	1994	1995	1996	1997	1998
All Children[1]	9,400	10,500	10,600	11,000	11,000	100	100	100	100	100
Sex										
Boys	5,500	6,200	6,300	6,600	6,600	59	59	59	60	60
Girls	3,900	4,300	4,300	4,400	4,400	41	41	41	40	40
Age[2]										
Under 1	170	200	160	170	160	2	2	1	2	1
1 to 4	1,500	1,500	1,400	1,300	1,100	16	14	13	12	10
5 to 9	2,700	3,000	3,100	3,200	3,200	29	29	30	29	29
10 to 15	3,700	4,200	4,400	4,800	4,900	39	40	41	43	45
16 and over	1,300	1,500	1,600	1,500	1,600	14	15	15	14	15
Average age (yrs : months)	10:5	10:7	10:8	10:10	11:1					
Reason for being looked after[3]										
Parents/families need relief										
– child with disabilities	4,600	5,100	5,400	5,600	5,800	49	49	50	51	50
– other	2,800	3,300	3,300	3,300	3,100	30	31	31	30	28
Parent's health	690	740	770	690	600	7	7	7	6	6
Child's welfare	370	430	310	370	360	4	4	3	3	3
Other	880	970	940	1,050	1,100	10	9	9	10	10

1 All children looked after under one or more agreed series of short term placements at any time during the year ending 31 March.

2 Age at the end of the latest episode of care, or at 31 March if child is still covered by an agreement

3 Reason for being looked after relate to child's latest episode of care during the year

Stability within the care of local authorities

Frequency of placement change

2.33   If children are not properly assessed when they first present for help, they may be wrongly placed and move through a variety of placements. This reduces the likelihood of their obtaining the stability and security they need.

2.34   Analysis of the number of placement changes children experience against how long they have been looked after shows:

- a high level of change in the first month - 39 placement changes per one hundred children

- a quick reduction in the number of placements per month to about 10 to 12 placement changes per month per 100 children for children looked after for longer than six months.

2.35   These are the national averages. There is, however, a very wide variation between authorities in the proportion of children who have three or more placements *in the first three months* of their being looked after. This ranges from below 5% to above 25%. The England average is 12%.

2.36   In order to tackle the problem of instability caused by changes of placement, the Government set a key target in *Modernising Health and Social Services: National Priorities Guidance 1999/00 to 2001/02*:

To reduce to no more than 16% in all authorities, by 2001, the number of children looked after who have three or more placements in one year.

2.37   The current variation between authorities in this indicator is illustrated in Figure 2.3. This indicator deals with all placements experienced by a child in a 12 month period, focusing on those who have had 3 or more. The figures, which are based on a one-third sample of looked after children in each authority, vary from 3% to 41%.

2.38   The target is calculated on the basis of the percentage all authorities would need to achieve by 2001 if they are to match the performance of the current top 25%. Some authorities face a considerable challenge. More than 30 authorities will need to reduce the proportion of their children with three or more placements by more than a third, and a few authorities will need to halve their current levels to achieve the target. Authorities will need to pay particular attention to the placement of young people aged 13 to 16 who tend to be over- represented in the group with three or more placements.

Figure 2.3 Children looked after at 31 March 1998 with three or more placements during the year, as a percentage of all children looked after at 31 March 1998, by local authority

percentage of all children looked after at 31 March 1998

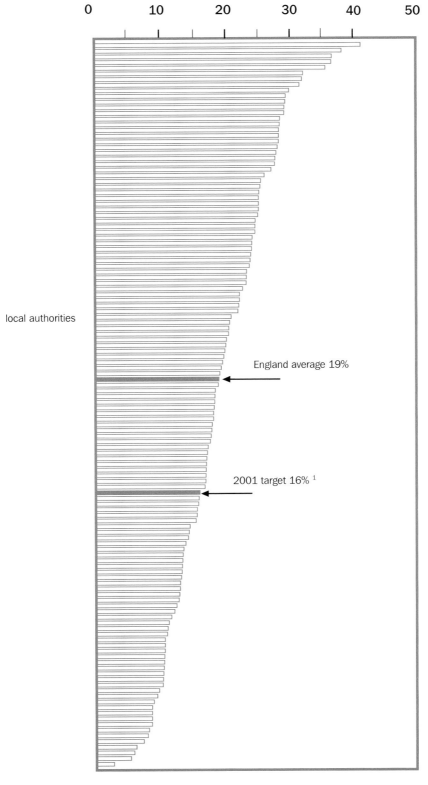

1 National Priorities Guidence target for each authority for year ending 31 March 2001

Figure 2.4 Children looked after at 31 March 1998 with three or more placements during the year, as a percentage of all children looked after at 31 March, by region

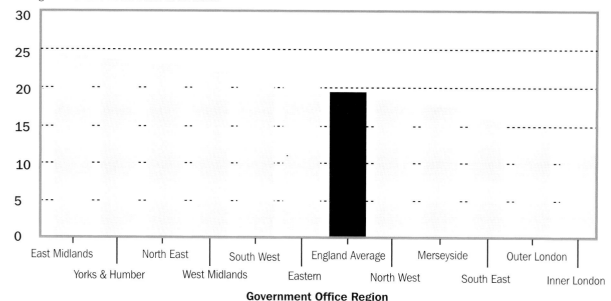

Percentage of all children looked after at 31 March

Government Office Region

2.39   Authorities in the south east of England tend to have lower rates for this indicator (Figure 2.4). This is even more marked in London, with the lowest figures in inner London. The reasons are not obvious. They may reflect limited placement options and the greater tendency to place children out of the authority area with the result that children are left where they are, even if this is less than satisfactory because there is no easy alternative.

2.40   The supply of placements for looked after children is discussed in Resource Planning (Chapter 9), where Tables 9.5 and 9.6 provide figures on the availability of placements in foster care and residential care.

2.41   In some cases, short term placements may be inevitable at the start of a period of care. These may be preferable to placement changes in the later stages of a period of care which might be less understandable to the child and therefore more damaging. It is for each authority to examine the local situation and seek to understand it in terms of their placement practices and supply of placements and to use that understanding to achieve improvement.

2.42   In summary, analysis of the data indicates that, in order to achieve the National Priorities Guidance target, many local authorities may need to concentrate on:

- new admissions
- young people aged 13 to 16
- placement practices and supply.

Time spent in a single placement

2.43   Another complementary way of looking at stability is to examine how long children who have been looked after for some time have remained with the same carers. Table 2.4 shows the proportion of children who have been looked after for four or more years who have been in their present placement for at least two years or who are placed for adoption.

2.44   These figures show that, on average, local authorities achieve foster placements lasting in excess of two years or an adoptive placement for half of the children who have been looked after for four or more years. For younger children the average percentage tends to be higher. There are a number of authorities who achieve significantly better and some authorities who fall far

Table 2.4 Children looked after at 31 March 1998 in foster placements or placed for adoption, who had been looked after continuously for at least four years, by age

England			numbers and percentages
	Number of children looked after for more than four years	Number of children who had been in their foster placements for at least 2 years, or who were placed for adoption	Percentage of children who had been in their foster placements for at least 2 years, or who were placed for adoption
All Children[1]	**15,200**	**7,800**	*51*
Age at 31 March 1998			
4	200	130	62
5	330	230	69
6	370	200	55
7	480	280	59
8	640	400	63
9	860	510	59
10	950	550	58
11	960	550	57
12	1,400	780	57
13	1,400	770	53
14	1,600	860	52
15	1,900	870	*47*
16	1,800	760	*41*
17	2,100	840	*41*

1   Excludes agreed series of short term placements

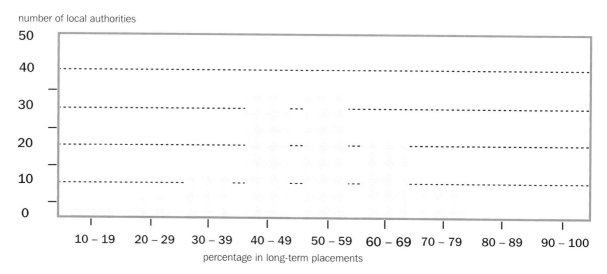

Figure 2.5 Percentage of children looked after at 31 March 1998 continuously for more than four years, who were in long term placements[1], in each local authority

[1] These are children looked after for more than 4 years who were placed for adoption at 31 March 1998, or who had been in their foster placement for at least 2 years

short of these average figures as can be seen in Figure 2.5. Authorities can ascertain where they stand by referring to Table 10 of the Children Looked After Statistics 1997-98, seek to understand the reasons and ask whether improvement is called for.

Messages from Inspection

When leaving care is leaving home: The Inspection of Leaving Care Services (1997) found:

- stability in a foster care placement was sometimes sacrificed to fit in with leaving care schemes

- some SSDs assumed that to be prepared for leaving statutory care meant changing placement to live in specialist resources. This led to foster carers being wary of services from leaving care teams.

The Duration of placements

2.45   Table 2.5 is an account of all placements made by all authorities during the course of the year ending 31 March 1997. It is important to bear in mind that the figures in this table represent placements not children. The figures show that nearly 94,000 individual placements of looked after children were made and that:

- about a quarter lasted less than eight days

- of these very short term placements, 75% were placements with foster carers. (This is somewhat higher than foster care's contribution to all placements - 68%)

- a further 13% were in children's homes

- the next largest group were placements with parents - about 6%.

2.46   Although placements in schools represent only about one and a half per cent of all placements, and it would be expected that such placements would have a longer term purpose, it seems that two thirds of placements in schools last under three months. This raises questions about the purpose of these placements and how they secure educational opportunities for the children they serve.

Table 2.5 Duration of placements ceasing during the year ending 31 March 1998[1]

England   numbers of placements

	All placements	1 - 7 days	8 days to under 1 month	1 month to under 3 months	3 months to under 6 months	6 months to under 1 year	1 year to under 2 years	2 years to under 5 years	5 year and ove
Placements	**90,500**	**22,400**	**17,500**	**15,200**	**10,600**	**11,000**	**8,100**	**4,300**	**1,500**
Foster placements	61,400	17,300	12,300	9,300	6,400	7,100	5,000	2,800	1,100
Children's homes	12,800	2,800	2,400	2,800	1,700	1,500	950	490	80
Schools	1,500	380	230	380	140	100	140	130	20
Placed with parents	5,700	730	790	990	900	800	750	540	160
Placed for adoption	1,700	10	20	60	200	510	600	210	50
In lodgings, living independently or in residential employment	2,800	310	530	620	540	480	300	30	-
Other placements	4,700	840	1,100	1,100	680	540	350	130	20

[1] Excludes agreed series of short term placements

**Figure 2.6 Placements lasting less than 8 days experienced by
children ceasing to be looked after during 1996/97[1]**

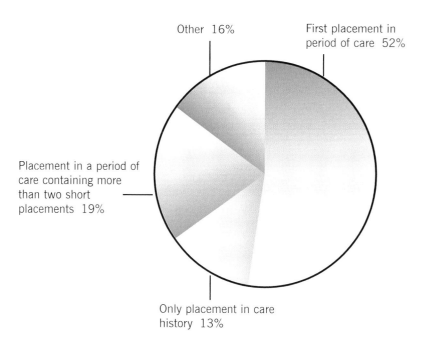

Other 16%

First placement in
period of care 52%

Placement in a period of
care containing more
than two short
placements 19%

Only placement in care
history 13%

1 Excludes placements forming part of agreed series of short term placements,
  and some temporary placements where the child returns to the previous
  placement

2.47   Figure 2.6 sheds some further light on how very short term placements (less
       than eight days) are used in the care of looked after children:

- slightly over half of these represent the child's initial placement during a
  period of care

- in only 13% does this represent the only placement before the child
  returns home

- but 19% of these very short placements represent a "staging posts" in a
  series of three or more placements during an episode of care. Most short
  placements with parents come into this category reflecting the use of
  "home on trial".

The contribution of adoption

2.48   Some 2000 children have been adopted out of local authority care each year in recent years. This figure has declined from a peak of about 2500 in 1993 (Figure 2.7) but increased in 1998 and again in 1999. All the evidence from research suggests that authorities do not attach sufficient priority to adoption. There is scope for further analysis of how adoption is being used to secure the future of children. The Department is commissioning urgent research on this question.

Figure 2.7 Number of looked after children adopted during years ending 31 March 1993 to 1999

number of children

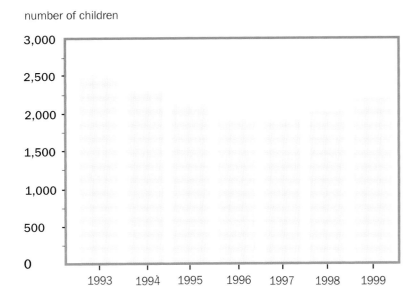

1 Method used to collect data for 1999 differed from that used in previous years, and therefore the figure may not be entirely consistent with earlier figures.

2.49   Over half of children adopted out of local authority care are less than five years old at adoption. As can be seen in Table 2.6, this proportion has increased in recent years.

2.50   Looked after children who are subsequently adopted tend to have more stable care histories than other looked after children. Most of those who go on to be adopted are looked after continuously from when they start to be looked after to when they are adopted. Of those adopted during 1996/97, more than 80% had uninterrupted care histories, compared with less than 70% of all children ceasing to be looked after during that year. 70% of children adopted during 1996/97 had three or fewer placements during their final (or only) period of care, including their final adoptive placement.

2.51   Some looked after children are adopted by the foster carers who had initially undertaken to care for them on a fostering basis only. Information from a survey of local authorities conducted by the British Association of Adoption and Fostering in 1998 suggests that 16% of children adopted from care were adopted by their former foster carers.

Table 2.6 Looked after children adopted[1] during the years ending 31 March 1994 to 1998

England   numbers and percentages

	numbers					percentages				
	1994	1995	1996	1997	1998	1994	1995	1996	1997	1998
All Children[2]	2,300	2,100	1,900	1,900	2,000	100	100	100	100	100
Sex										
Boys	1,200	1,000	990	930	1,000	51	50	51	50	51
Girls	1,100	1,000	940	950	980	49	50	49	50	49
Age at adoption										
Under 1	210	210	150	140	150	9	10	8	8	7
1 to 4	910	830	870	890	1,000	40	40	45	47	47
5 to 9	790	700	620	590	630	34	34	32	31	31
10 to 15	340	290	260	220	160	15	14	14	12	12
16 and over	50	30	30	30	30	2	2	1	2	1
Average age (yrs:months)	5:11	5:9	5:6	5:5	4:11					

1 Children who ceased to be looked after, where "adopted" was given as the reason final episode ceased
2 Figures for children looked after in this table exclude agreed series of short term placements

2.52   Figure 2.8 shows that a greater proportion of adopted children became looked after because of abuse or neglect than is the case with all children ceasing to be looked after - 45% compared with 22%. This is to be expected if good child care planning and decision making is operating. However, some 5% of adopted children entered the public care because parents needed relief. This is, on the face of it, a surprising figure. It no doubt masks the complexity of individual cases and the unfolding of events. But it also raises questions about how clear social workers are about their reasons for arranging for children to be looked after. The quality of assessment and the consequent validity of classification is an issue highlighted in several parts of this report.

Figure 2.8 Looked after children adopted during 1997/98 and all children ceasing to be looked after during 1997/98, by reason for starting to be looked after[1]

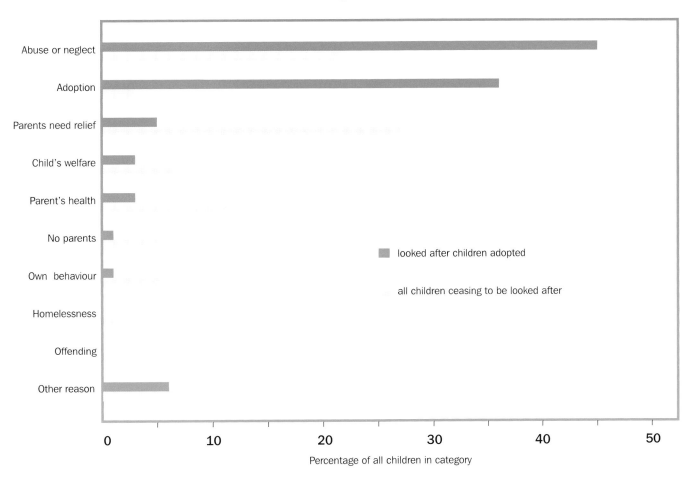

Percentage of all children in category

1 Excludes children where no reason was recorded

2.53 Table 2.7 gives a clear indication of the time it takes to secure adoptions for looked after children. This varies very significantly with the legal status of the child which, in turn, probably reflects the complexity of children's circumstances. It shows that from the time the child is looked after to the making of the adoption order:

- children who are adopted most quickly are those who are looked after by agreement with their parents (under Section 20). They are adopted on average within 2 years of becoming looked after. However the proportion of these children, to all children adopted, has reduced from 22 to 16% in the five years from 1994-98

- over the same 5 year period, the proportion of children freed for adoption increased from 21 to 32%; these are adopted on average in just over three years

- those who are looked after on care orders take longest to be adopted – about four years. They constitute the greatest proportion of looked after children and are likely to have needed protection through court proceedings because of neglect or abuse.

Table 2.7 Looked after children adopted during the years ending 31 March 1994 to 1998 by legal status on adoption and time being looked after[1]

England			numbers, percentages and durations	
	Number of children	Percentage of adoptions in the year	Average time looked after *before adoption*	
			years	months
All children[2]				
1994	2,300	*100*	3	6
1995	2,100	*100*	3	7
1996	1,900	*100*	3	6
1997	1,900	*100*	3	4
1998	2,000	*100*	3	3
Care orders				
1994	1,300	*57*	4	2
1995	1,100	*52*	4	4
1996	980	*51*	4	1
1997	950	*51*	4	0
1998	1,000	*52*	3	11
Section 20 CA 1989				
1994	500	*22*	2	1
1995	470	*23*	2	1
1996	380	*20*	2	1
1997	330	*18*	1	11
1998	320	*16*	1	9
Freed for adoption				
1994	490	*21*	3	3
1995	530	*25*	3	5
1996	570	*29*	3	3
1997	590	*31*	3	0
1998	640	*32*	3	0

1 Includes a small number of children for whom details of care histories before the implementation of the Children Act are not available. Excludes agreed series of short term placements.

2 Includes a small number of children under other legal statuses

2.54 These figures for the period of time between becoming looked after and being adopted are consistent from year to year. They show that the need for court intervention to resolve issues arising out of complexity of the case or the resistance of children's parents to the adoption plan is one of the major determinants of the time it takes to achieve adoption. Another factor is, of course, the time it takes for a local authority to come to a decision that adoption is in the best interest of the child. The Department of Health is examining ways of obtaining information about this and introducing performance indicators on the length of time children are in care before adoption.

Messages from Inspection

Two adoption reports, *"For Children's Sake: An SSI Inspection of Local Authority Adoption Services"* and *Part II "An Inspection of Local Authority Post-Placement And Post-Adoption Services"* (1996 and 1997) identified a number of problems in relation to adoption services. They found:

- Children's Services Plans provided a good planning framework but reference to adoption was peripheral. It was not promoted as a care option

- strategic oversight of adoption services varied considerably and comprehensive adoption services were not implemented in some areas

- a risk of diminishing expertise due to inadequate attention being paid to adoption by SSDs

- little attention was given to the outcomes of adoption and few were able to evaluate its worth as a care option

- one of the major findings of both inspections was that adoption for many children was an unnecessarily lengthy process. This resulted from:

    unclear or over optimistic assessments of birth families' parenting skills;

    prolonged court proceedings;

    insufficient direct work with children, ensuring their real involvement in plans;

    overlong - if sound - assessment processes for adopters;

    insufficient monitoring of children and adopters awaiting placement.

- a lack of monitoring of the time taken for adoption; many SSDs did not know how long adoptions were taking and were, thus, unable to take specific action to reduce delay.

2.55 Improvements in adoption services are a key aim of the Quality Protects programme. New performance indicators are being set. Statistical collections will be improved. SSI will conduct a nationwide survey and a major inspection in the coming year. Future Children Act reports will discuss the impact of these developments.

Child Protection

Objective: To ensure that children are protected from emotional, physical, sexual abuse and neglect (significant harm)

Introduction

3.1 The Children Act requires children's welfare to be both safeguarded and promoted. As part of ensuring children's healthy development it is crucial that they are protected from abuse - physical, sexual, emotional - and neglect.

3.2 The safeguarding and promoting of children's welfare is as important for children looked after by local authorities as it is for those being brought up in their own families.

3.3 *"The Children Act says that the first duty of a local authority to a child it is looking after is 'to safeguard and promote his welfare.... 'Safeguard ' and 'promote' are equal partners in an overall concept of welfare. Safeguards are an indispensable component to the child's security, and should be the first consideration for any body providing or arranging accommodation for children. Safeguards form the basis for ensuring physical and emotional health, good education and sound development".* (People Like us. paras 1. 22-23).

3.4 Data does not exist on the actual numbers of children being maltreated at any one time. Estimates from various studies suggest the following rates of annual incidence per 1,000 children.

Types of Abuse	Annual Incidence
Physical	3.5
Sexual	2.0
Emotional	3.0
Neglect	14.6

3.5 National statistics, which relate to the registration of children's names on child protection registers provides one way of assessing performance in this area. However, the statistics relating to child protection registers do not, by definition, include all children known to suffer significant harm. In addition they are known to be strongly influenced by local policy, procedures and context. They are not, therefore, a reliable indicator of the actual levels of maltreatment children suffer in a particular locality.

Basic information on children on the child protection register

Table 3.1 Registrations, de-registrations and numbers on the child protection register at 31 March, 1988 to 1998			
England			numbers
	On the register at 31 March	Registrations during the year	De-registrations during the year
1988	39,200	20,900	17,900
1989	41,200	23,000	21,800
1990	43,600	26,900	24,200
1991	45,300	28,300	26,700
1992	38,600	24,500	31,300
1993	32,500	24,700	29,400
1994	34,900	28,500	26,200
1995	35,000	30,400	30,200
1996	32,400	28,300	30,500
1997	32,400	29,200	28,900
1998	31,600	30,000	30,200

3.6   Table 3.1 illustrates the marked changes in numbers of registrations and de-registrations from year to year. There was a substantial reduction in the numbers of children's names on registers between 1991 and 1993. The marked drop in the years following 1991 was linked to the discontinuation of the 'grave concern' category in Working Together guidance issued to coincide with the implementation of the Children Act. The Department intends to find ways of producing more reliable statistics on child protection activity.

3.7   There is further exploration of the variation between authorities in rates of registration in Chapter 9.

3.8   Rates of registration also went down from 1995-1996 which coincided with the publication of 'Child Protection – Messages from Research'. Research had shown that, in some circumstances, children were being registered inappropriately as a means of obtaining access to supportive services. Subsequently, national policy has promoted the message that children's services should look widely at the needs of vulnerable children and families. While there should remain a clear focus on safeguarding children at risk of significant harm, children and their families should not be subject to child protection procedures as a means of securing access to services. Other important messages from this research programme included:

- over half of the estimated 160,000 or so children who are each year subject to child protection enquiries under Section 47 receive no further services once the enquiry has been completed

- enquiries into suspicions of child abuse can have traumatic effects on families. Good professional practice can ease parents' anxiety and lead to co-operation that helps to protect the child. Professionals could do more to work in partnership with parents and the child

- while inter-agency work is often relatively good at the early stages of child protection enquiries, its effectiveness tends to decline once child protection plans have been made, with social services left with sole responsibility for implementing these plans

- discussions at child protection conferences tend to focus too heavily on decisions about registration and removal rather than focusing on plans to protect the child and support the family

- there is inconsistent use of the child protection register which is not consulted for 60% of children for whom there is some child protection concern.

3.9   The Department subsequently announced its intention to revise *'Working Together under the Children Act 1989'*, which forms inter-departmental guidance on how agencies should co-operate to protect children from abuse and neglect. A consultation document was published in 1998, and new guidance *"Working Together to Safeguard Children"* published in consultative draft form in August 1999 for England and Wales.

3.10 The key message which the Government wishes to promote is a new emphasis on looking more widely at the needs of the most vulnerable children and families in communities. Many of the families who find themselves caught up in the child protection system suffer from multiple disadvantages. They need help at an earlier stage to tackle their problems before parenting difficulties escalate into crisis or abuse. Assessment of the needs of children and their families will be key to providing better targeted support.

3.11 However, the Government recognises that an effective child protection system will continue to be needed to deal with cases of abuse or neglect. There is commitment to reinforcing the best elements of the existing child protection system and no intention of destabilising those elements which work well. The new guidance will need to keep a clear focus on securing good outcomes for children as a result of child protection interventions. It will aim to identify clearly the key principles and practices which Government expects to be followed.

3.12 Work on the new guidance has been informed by increased understanding and knowledge in many areas of child abuse which have taken place over the past decade. There is now a better understanding of the problem of child sexual abuse and its long-term adverse effects on the welfare and development of children. More is known about the methods that sex offenders employ to gain access to children. The extent and seriousness of abuse suffered by some children in residential care in the 1970s and 1980s was far greater than previously understood. *People Like us*, Sir William Utting's report of the review of safeguards for children living away from home, published in November 1997, identified major faults in the care and safeguards provided for these children. The Government announced the establishment of a Ministerial Task Force to develop a full programme of policy and management changes to deliver a safer environment. The new guidance will play its part in ensuring effective child protection procedures.

Messages from inspection

Responding to Families in Need: The Inspection of Assessment, Planning and Decision - Making in Family Support Services (1997) found:

- decisions about how cases should be classified were being taken on the basis of inadequate assessments, made by sometimes very inexperienced and usually overworked staff

- some children were being left in neglectful situations for too long while too many other children were the subject of unnecessary enquiries (under Section 47)

- poorly developed eligibility criteria or associated guidance about priorities. This meant staff made choices without guidance or had their own interpretations of the criteria.

Registrations by category of abuse

3.13   Figure 3.1 shows that numbers of children being registered under the categories of physical and sexual abuse are decreasing whilst those under emotional abuse and neglect are increasing both in actual numbers and as a proportion of all registrations. This trend may be related to local authorities being clearer in their understanding of the impact of the neglect and emotional abuse on children's health and development. They may be using them instead of the "grave concern" category the use of which was no longer recommended in 1991. The picture is clearly complex. A recent inspection found continuing staff uncertainties in the assessment and identification of emotional abuse which suggests that emotional abuse is under-identified and therefore would be under-represented on child protection registers.

Figure 3.1 Percentage of registrations to child protection registers during the years ending 31 March 1994 to 1998, by category of abuse

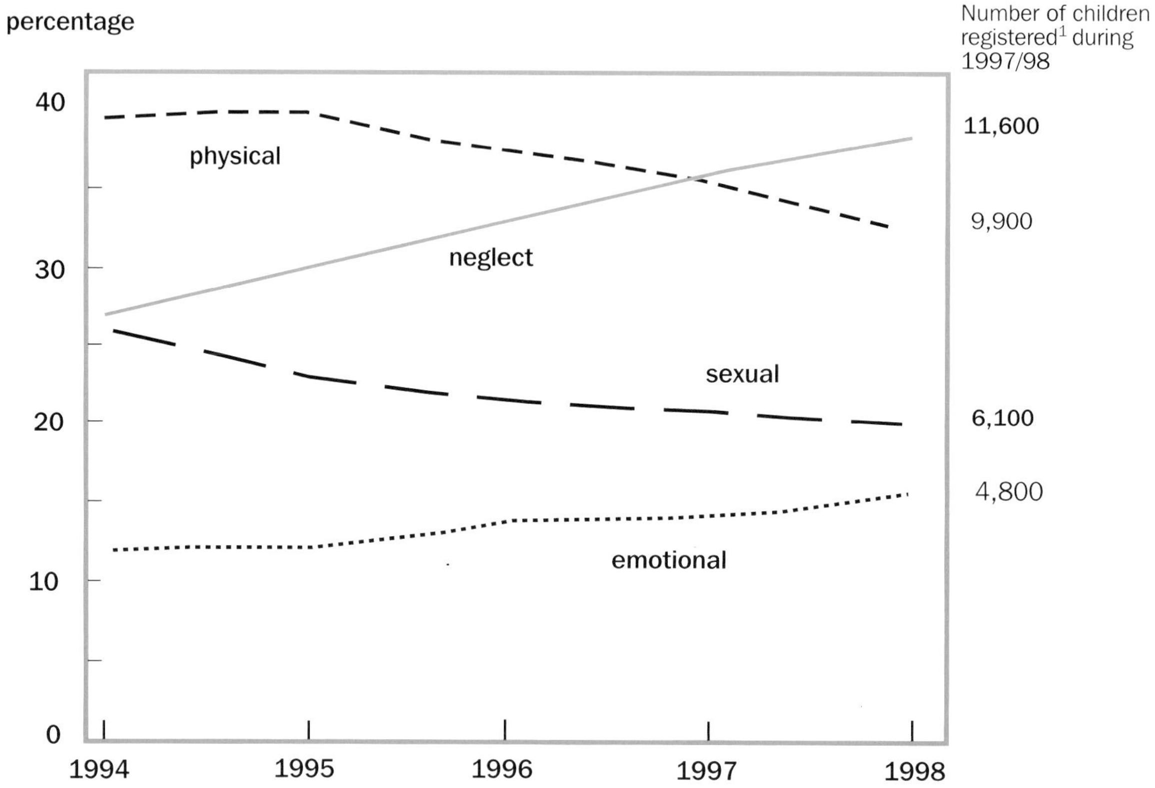

percentage

Number of children registered[1] during 1997/98

1 Some children appear in more than one category; the total therefore exceeds the number of registrations in Table 3.1

Messages from Inspection

Getting Family Support Right: The Inspection of the Delivery of Family Support Services (1999) found:

- examples where indicators of abuse had either not been understood or identified

- uncertainty about the threshold for initiating child protection enquiries, particularly among family centre staff dealing with complex family situations but lacking sufficient training and guidance in child protection

- uncertainty and confusion about what constituted emotional abuse.

Re-registrations – children placed on child protection registers more than once

3.14   A child's name remains on a child protection register until it is agreed by a review child protection conference that an inter-agency child protection plan is no longer required to safeguard the child from significant harm. Effective intervention when a child's name is on the register should result in fewer re-registrations. This means that focused interventions result in changes in the family functioning such that the parents and significant others in the child's family can ensure their safety and enable them to develop and thrive. There will be a need to re-register some children where it had been appropriate to de-register their names, but where, since doing so, their family circumstances have changed in ways that put them at risk of significant harm, which could not have been anticipated in advance. There will be other situations, which are of concern, where re-registration is the result of ineffective or insufficient intervention and where the required family changes did not take place. Rates of re-registration should provide some indication of the effectiveness of:

- social services interventions, in concert with other agencies, to bring about the required change within the family system; and

- the child protection plan in ensuring optimal outcomes for the child, dependent on sufficient change taking place within the family's patterns of functioning and parenting capacity.

Table 3.2 Numbers of registrations to child protection registers during the years ending 31 March 1992 to 1998, by whether first registrations or re-registrations

England   numbers and percentages

		number of registrations		percentages	
	Number of registrations	First registrations	Re-registrations	First registrations	Re-registrations
1992	24,500	21,600	2,900	88	12
1993	24,700	21,100	3,600	85	15
1994	28,500	23,900	4,600	84	16
1995	30,400	25,700	4,700	84	16
1996	28,300	23,200	5,100	82	18
1997	29,200	23,600	5,600	81	19
1998	30,000	24,200	5,800	81	19

3.15   Table 3.2 shows a steady increase between 1992 and 1998 from 12 to 19% in the proportion of registrations which are re-registrations and a doubling of the actual numbers. This suggests that interventions, whilst the children's names are on the register, are not resulting in long-term changes to the capacity of parents to keep their children safe and enable them to thrive. It is, however, also the case that re-registration occurs appropriately, because of new concerns that arise following apparently successful earlier interventions.

3.16   In order to improve the quality of work undertaken with children and families, when the child's name is on the register, the following indicator was chosen as a National Priorities Guidance target.

Reduce by 10%, by 2002, the proportion of children who are re-registered on the child protection register, from a baseline for the year ending March 1997.

3.17   It is recognised that some authorities are achieving this target and have few re-registrations currently. Family situations can and do change quickly over time. Some re-registrations are to be expected therefore and will be appropriate for the needs of the child.

Figure 3.2 Percentage of re-registrations to the child protection register during the year ending 31 March 1998, by local authority

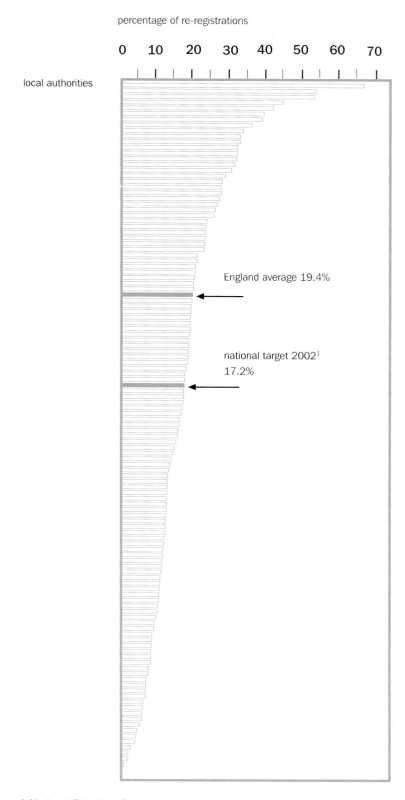

1 National Priorities Guidence target for England average for year
  ending 31 March 2002

Table 3.3 Numbers and percentages of children de-registered from child protection registers during the years ending 31 March 1994 to 1998

England   numbers and percentages

		numbers					percentages				
		length of time on register					length of time on register				
	All children	Under 3 months	3 months to under 6 months	6 months to under 1 year	1 year to under 2 years	2 years & over	Under 3 months	3 months to under 6 months	6 months to under 1 year	1 year to under 2 years	2 years & over
1994	26,200	1,900	4,700	7,600	6,500	5,400	7	18	29	25	21
1995	30,200	2,100	5,500	9,400	8,000	5,200	7	18	31	26	17
1996	30,500	2,100	5,500	9,500	8,800	4,600	7	18	31	29	15
1997	28,900	2,100	5,700	9,000	8,100	4,100	7	20	31	28	14
1998	30,200	2,200	5,800	9,900	8,300	4,000	7	19	33	27	13

3.18   Table 3.3 shows that from 1994 to 1998 there was a reduction from 21% to 13% in the proportion of children who have been on the child protection register for more than two years. Analysis of the data suggests that there is a significant negative correlation between re-registrations and the proportion of de-registrations that are of children who have been on the register a long time. That is, high re-registrations tend to be in authorities which have low proportions of children on the register for more than two years and vice-versa. The analysis shows that:

- virtually no authorities have high re-registration rates and high rates for long duration on the register

- but, on the other hand, many authorities achieve low re-registrations and low duration rates.

3.19   This implies that it may not be necessary to increase the average periods of time children's names remain on child protection registers in order to reduce re-registration rates and hence contribute to the National Priorities Guidance target. To ensure children are being kept safe and thriving, local authorities must in each case consider, on the basis of evidence, what type of therapeutic help is made available to children and their families in order to ensure that underlying problems are addressed by the appropriate kind of intervention

3.20   Because of the inter-relationship between re-registration rates and the duration of periods children spend on registers, it is, therefore, sensible to assess how an authority is performing by looking at a set of indicators in conjunction with re-registration, namely the:

- numbers on the register at a given time

- rates of registrations and de-registrations

- proportion of registrations which are re-registrations and

- duration of children's names being on the register.

The use of Care Orders and Supervision Orders to intervene to safeguard the welfare of children

3.21   In some situations, placing a child's name on the child protection register and implementing a child protection plan whilst the child remains living with the parents, may be insufficient to ensure the child's safety. Where a child is found to be suffering significant harm, or be likely to in the future, consideration should be given to whether the grounds are met for initiating court proceedings under Section 31 of the Children Act. There is, however, no statistical way of associating the numbers of child protection enquiries or children's names placed on the child protection register with the numbers of care orders made.

Table 3.4 Numbers of children starting[1] to be looked after under care orders and numbers of children placed under supervision orders (S31 CA 1989), years ending 31 March 1993 to 1998

England						numbers
	1993	1994	1995	1996	1997	1998
Children starting to be looked after under Care Orders[1]	1,800	2,400	3,000	3,100	3,200	4,600
Full	700	600	750	690	580	1,100
Interim	1,100	1,800	2,200	2,400	2,600	3,500
Children placed under Supervision Orders (S31 CA 1989)[2]	2,130	2,640	2,610	2,550	2,200	..
Full	1,420	1,340	1,520	1,620	1,530	..
Interim	710	1,300	1,090	930	670	..

1   Only the first occasion on which a child started to be looked after in the year has been counted

2   These figures are no longer collected by the Department of Health

..   not available

3.22   Table 3.4 shows a clear trend, during the period 1993 to 1998, of increasing numbers and proportion of children for whom care orders have been necessary to secure their health and development. This implies that there has been a shift towards interventions sanctioned by the courts. This trend is most apparent in the increased use of both interim and full care orders between 1997 and 1998. There has been a less pronounced increase in the numbers of children placed on child protection registers during the same period but the increase in the use of care orders to safeguard children's welfare is more marked.

3.23   There has been no discernible trend in relation to the use of supervision orders.

3.24   The significance of the trend is further illuminated by findings from research and by considering the cost implications of court action. Firstly, research has established that better outcomes are achieved through working, wherever possible, in partnership with parents. Secondly, the cost of taking cases to court is undoubtedly higher than action taken on the basis of agreement with parents. For both these reasons, hard-pressed social service departments would not be expected to take care proceedings without there being good grounds for doing so. The figures suggest that local authorities are seeking the authority of a court order in situations where parents will not voluntarily co-operate with a child protection plan, or do not have the capacity to respond appropriately to their children's needs, and the making of a care order is the best way of securing their safety, and ensuring their health and development.

Allocation of a social worker

3.25   Having an allocated social worker is an important element in child protection. The proportion of looked after children with an allocated social worker is one of the indicators local authorities are asked to look at in the Quality Protects Management Action Plans.

Messages from Inspection

Someone Else's Children: The Inspections of Planning and Decision - Making for Children Looked After and The Safety of Children Looked After (1998) *found:*

- most social service departments gave priority to looked after children in allocating social workers but

- out of the 27 authorities inspected 3 had problems of unallocated cases

- one of those authorities had 26% of its cases unallocated

- another authority could not provide data.

Life Chances of Children in Need

Objective: To ensure that gain maximum life chance benefits from educational opportunities, health care and social care.

Who are children in need?

4.1   Section 17(10) of the Children Act 1989 defines children in need as those whose standard of health or development is likely to be impaired unless they receive social services, or if they are disabled.

4.2   'Children in Need' represent a population of children who are hard to identify rigorously for statistical purposes. They include children looked after by local authorities, who in their own right are relatively easy to identify, but represent only about 13% of the total. There is no administrative process uniformly required to identify a child as being 'in need'. It is, therefore, difficult to measure both the extent of local authority activity in this area and to assess its effectiveness.

4.3   Currently we can only estimate the numbers of children in need in terms of the numbers of children receiving services. A survey carried out by the MORI/York University/National Children's Bureau consortium in 1996 provided the basis for an estimate of 350,000 children in need at any one time who were known to social services departments in England. That is about 3% of all children.

4.4   The Department of Health has piloted, and is planning to introduce in the latter part of the 1999/2000 financial year, a new collection of expenditure on children in need based on a week's census of activity. This will provide new estimates of the numbers of children in need served by local authorities broken down into classifications of need, the services they receive and the distribution of expenditure incurred.

4.5   However, many agencies, other than social services, work with children who have a range of difficulties deserving attention - for example, schools and health visitors. Not all of these children will be referred to social services. It may therefore be necessary to recognise another group of children who require help from a variety of agencies, other than social services. Although the children have needs, they are not technically 'children in need'. It may be appropriate to describe these children as 'children at risk of social exclusion'. Children in need are a subset of children at risk of social exclusion and are children who need personal social services under Part III of the Children Act.

4.6 The requirement to plan services for children in education, juvenile justice and health has thrown into relief the problems of understanding the scope and limitations of the term "children in need". The Department intends to clarify the meaning of a children in need within the context of policy to combat social exclusion in a forthcoming new assessment framework and guidance on Children's Services Planning. As was discussed in *Modernising Social Services*, it is the government's intention that Children's Services Plans should bring together action planned at local level by a range of agencies on behalf of the main groups of children at risk of social exclusion.

4.7 Below we briefly discuss four areas concerning the welfare of children where a social exclusion perspective is particularly appropriate.

Young Carers

4.8 It is important that children and young people who provide personal care for their chronically sick or disabled parents or siblings are not expected to carry inappropriate levels of caring which impact on their development and thereby serve to limit their life chances. Parents may need support to maintain their independence and carry out their parenting responsibilities. There may be a delicate balance to be struck between the rights of children to have support to reduce their caring burden and the reluctance of some families to accept intervention or support from social services. Co-operation with other agencies such as health, education and voluntary sectors and also between adult's and children's services within social services departments, is vital to overcome such issues. Services providing support should not undermine the parent's ability to parent or make the child feel that he or she has failed.

4.9 Young carers can receive help from both local and health authorities. Children providing a substantial amount of care on a regular basis for a parent, are entitled to an assessment of their ability to cope under Section 1(1) of the Carers (Recognition and Services) Act 1995. Local authorities are obliged to take such assessments into account in deciding what community care services to provide for the parents. A young carer may be a child in need under the Children Act. The key issue is whether the child's welfare or development might suffer if support is not provided to the child or family. As part of the National Strategy for Carers, local authorities are required to identify children with additional family burdens and to provide services that are geared to ensure these children's health, education and general development do not suffer.

School Inclusion

4.10 The role of schools in helping children at risk of social exclusion, and the importance of good local multi-agency working, are highlighted in the guidance "Social Inclusion: Pupil Support" which was issued by DfEE in July 1999 as part of the response to the Social Exclusion Unit's report on Truancy and School Exclusion. The guidance explains the law and gives examples of good practice on matters such as school attendance, pupil behaviour and discipline, and school exclusion, all of which - if not properly managed - can lead to social exclusion. A child's deportment at school can also offer indicators of problems elsewhere. The guidance accordingly underlines the importance of schools being aware of a child's home circumstances, and of liaison with other agencies, including social services, where necessary to identify and ensure a joined-up response to the child's needs. The over-riding emphasis is on prevention and intervention at an early stage to try and prevent more serious problems arising. The new assessment framework (Chapter 8) will make an important contribution.

Child and adolescent mental health

4.11   The Department's strategy for the development of child and adolescent mental health services (CAMHS) was set out in the National Priorities Guidance for Health and Social Services 1999/2002, issued to authorities last September. The overall requirement is to improve provision of appropriate, high-quality care and treatment for children and young people by building up locally-based CAMHS. This is to be achieved through improved staffing levels and training provision at all tiers and improved liaison between primary care, specialised CAMHS, social services and other agencies. An additional investment of £84 million over three years from the NHS Modernisation Fund and Mental Health Grant to support this development was recently announced and detailed guidance about the funding has been issued to health and local authorities.

Youth Offending

4.12   Under the Children Act 1989, local authorities have a statutory responsibility to take reasonable steps to reduce the need to bring criminal proceedings against children in their area and to encourage them not to commit criminal offences.

4.13   The Crime and Disorder Act 1998 establishes preventing offending by children and young people as the principal aim of the youth justice system and places a statutory duty on all those working in the system to have regard to that aim. To ensure that young offenders are dealt with effectively, the Act requires local authorities with social services and education responsibilities, in partnership with the police, probation service and health authorities and trusts, to establish inter-agency youth offending teams in their areas, for delivering youth justice services. Youth Offending Teams and the new orders introduced in the Crime and Disorder Act 1998 are currently being piloted and will be introduced nationally from April 2000.

4.14   To provide a clear national leadership in order to improve the performance of the youth justice system, the Youth Justice Board for England and Wales has been established to advise Ministers on setting standards for service delivery and to monitor performance. In this capacity, the Board will be collecting and publishing information from the authorities.

4.15 Because a significant amount of crime is unreported and a substantial amount of reported crime is not cleared up, it is not possible to present an accurate picture of the trends in the nature and extent of crime committed by children and young people aged 10 to 17 years. However, statistics produced by the Home Office show that the overall offending rate per 100,000 population among males aged 10 to 17 years cautioned or convicted of an offence, decreased from 7,500 in 1985 to 5,300 in 1997. Over the same period, among females aged 10 to 17 years, the proportion cautioned or convicted of an offence remained fairly steady.

4.16 In its report *"Misspent Youth: Young People and Crime"* published in 1996, the Audit Commission pointed out that the known rate of offending by young males aged 18 to 24 years had increased significantly. The most recent statistics produced by the Home Office for 1997 show that the peak age of known offending for females is now the same as males at 18 years of age, the first year of adulthood. Discouraging offending behaviour by children and young people before it becomes firmly established is, therefore, more important than ever.

How do we measure life chances?

4.17 There is less difficulty in identifying what all children need to acquire to promote their life chances than there is defining children in need. The research on which the report of the Department of Health Working Party *Looking After Children: Assessing Outcomes in Childcare* (1991) was based suggested there is a strong consensus about this. The seven dimensions of development identified in the report have been developed into the system of monitoring the well-being of looked after children but they apply equally to all children. They are:

- how well the children are doing in their education

- their health

- their emotional and behavioural development

- their sense of identity and self esteem

- their relationships with family and friends

- how well they fit in socially and

- whether they are acquiring the practical skills they need to look after themselves.

4.18 If parents or carers have the necessary parenting capacity, they will recognise that they want their children to progress in these areas. This can form the basis of an alliance between the social worker, the family and, often, other agencies for working out how to help the child to make desirable progress and, in so doing improve their life chances.

4.19 Thresholds for social services involvement in relation to 'children in need' are rarely well defined. There are undoubtedly large numbers of children who may barely register on the records of social services departments but who may have received crucial help when this was needed - perhaps through a piece of advice to their parents, or referral to day care provision or advice centre. There are others who are more formally recognised as 'cases' but where the intervention may be very short term, lasting perhaps just two or three weeks and then ceasing. The contact may be recorded but the records are not systematically collected to allow for aggregation. There is, therefore, no information on the volume of this activity.

4.20   Nor is it clear whether a child who needs *ad hoc* or short term help continues thereafter to be classified as a "Child in Need" or whether this applies only for the duration of the particular problem or the duration of the service. These are problematic issues *only* if one is trying to measure the impact of social service help on their lives.

Possible approaches to measuring outcomes for children in need but not looked after

4.21   Finding ways of measuring this objective is difficult and further work is necessary on how best to achieve this. Two approaches are feasible. It may, in future, be possible to define a group of children who receive a substantial level of help from personal social services and take steps to assess their developmental progress with respect to a set of indicators such as educational attainment, health or the acquisition of age appropriate practical skills. However, this will require significant developments in the recording of assessment and outcomes for children in need and is some way off. Furthermore it would not be easy to attribute the outcomes to work undertaken by the personal social services because the work of several other agencies may impact on the child. Work with children in need is essentially multi-agency even if social services occupy a central role.

4.22   Alternatively it might be more immediately feasible, as well as more in accord with a corporate approach to the care and development of children, if local authorities measured the well being of all the children in their communities against a common set of indicators published at local and national level. Progress made over time would reflect how all agencies work together to promote the life chances of children and young people in their areas. The aim should be, in particular, to improve the life chances of those children who are most disadvantaged or at risk of social exclusion. This would inevitably include a high proportion of children in need.

4.23   Table 4.1 provides a set of national average indicators, which might form the basis of such local comparisons. It is included as signalling a possible way ahead. Some of this thinking has been incorporated in the revised set of the Government's objectives and sub-objectives. A table such as this could be published annually in these reports and would enable local agencies, through children's services planning mechanisms, to set and monitor local targets for year on year improvements.

Table 4.1 Education, health and offending; a summary of data available for all children in England

Educational attainment by the end of 1997/98 school year (Source: DfEE)

GCSE/GNVQ achievements by 15 year old pupils[1] [2]

Percentage who achieved at GCSE or GNVQ equivalent at least:-

5+ A*– C grade	46
5+ A*– G grade	88
1+ A*– C grade	71
1+ A*– G grade	93

Percentage who achieved no qualifications at GCSE or GNVQ equivalent	7

Pupils absent from school, 1997/98 school year (Source: DfEE)

Average number of half days missed per absent pupil in maintained primary schools

Authorised absence	19
Unauthorised absence	10

Average number of half days missed per absent pupil in maintained secondary schools

Authorised absence	26
Unauthorised absence	20

Permanent exclusions from school, 1996/97 school year (Source: DfEE)

Number of permanent exclusions	12,668
Percentage of school population	0.2

Teenage pregnancies/births 1996 (Source: ONS)

Number of conceptions for under 16 year olds	8,200
Under 16 conception rates per 1,000 females	9.3
Percentage of pregnancies terminated by abortion, for under 16 year olds	52

Take-up of immunisations 1998 (Source: Department of Health)

Percentage of children immunised by their 2nd birthday[3]

Diphtheria/tetanus/polio	96
Pertussis (whooping cough)	94
Measles/mumps/rubella	91
Haemophilus influenzae b	95

Accident rates 1995-1997 combined (Source: Department of Health)

Annual accident rates for 2 – 15 year olds, per 10,000 population[4]

Boys

major	3,100
minor	21,600

Girls

major	2,200
minor	14,400

Table 4.1   Education, health and offending; a summary of data available for all children in England

Table 4.1 continued

Offending rates 1996 (Source: Home Office)
Young persons found guilty or cautioned for offences (excluding summary motoring),
per 10,000 population in the age group:-

Boys, aged

10 - 17	547
10 - 13	189
14 - 17	914

Girls, aged

10 - 17	139
10 - 13	62
14 - 17	218

1 Pupils on roll aged 15 at the start of the 1997/98 academic year, ie 31 August 1997
2 Including attempts and achievements by these pupils in previous academic years
3 Denominator – total number of children resident in England on 31 March 1998 reaching their 2nd birthday during the previous year
Numerator – total included in the above completing a primary course (3 doses except MMR) at any time up to their 2nd birthday
4 Accidents are classed as either major or minor. An accident is 'major' where professional help or advice was obtained. An accident is 'minor' where no professional help or advice was needed, but where pain and discomfort was experienced for at least 24 hours

Messages from Inspection

Responding to Families in Need: The Inspection of Assessment, Planning and Decision-making in Family Support Services (1997) found:

- poorly developed eligibility criteria for access, used to exclude rather than make services more readily available

- a lack of clear guidance for delegated decision-making and an absence of monitoring systems and management action to achieve consistency

- poor communication between managers and staff about how work was to be done

- most SSDs were developing a wide range of services

- Child and Adolescent Mental Health Services social workers were particularly effective at meeting the needs of the majority of users of this joint service.

Getting Family Support Right: The Inspection of the Delivery of Family Support Services (1999) found a much more positive situation in relation to services provided. It found:

- 80% of families were satisfied with their family support services

- parents felt supported, valued and well-informed, and shared an understanding about the purpose of the work

- however, in 40% of cases, there was inadequate recognition of indicators of child abuse and neglect and more understanding of the impact of emotional abuse was needed.

Life Chances of Children Looked After

Objective: To ensure that children looked after gain maximum life chance benefits from educational opportunities, health care and social care.

Introduction

5.1   "Looked after" is the term used in the Act to describe all children who are the subject of a care order, or who are provided with accommodation on a voluntary basis for more than 24 hours. A care order may only be made by a court.

5.2   Section 22 of the Children Act provides the basis for the 'corporate parent' role of local authorities who look after or accommodate a child by requiring them to:

- safeguard and promote his or her welfare and

- make use of other services which are available to children living with their parents which he or she needs.

5.3   There should be no difference in aspirations for looked after children than for all children. This objective is therefore the same as for children in need. Key differences are that looked after children constitute a clearly defined group and that there is a means of measuring their progress through the Looking After Children Action and Assessment records.

5.4   Another key difference from children in need is that information is available on how looked after children compare with all children on a number of indicators. They do not do nearly as well and concern for this state of affairs has been a key driver behind the Quality Protects programme.

Educational attainment

5.5   The single most important indicator of children's life chances is educational attainment. The unacceptable state of affairs in educational attainment of children looked after is reflected in the target chosen for the National Priorities Guidance. The limited amount of information on the educational attainment of looked after children from research studies and a pilot survey suggest that in some authorities, as few as a quarter of children leaving care at 16 or older with any GCSE or GNVQ qualifications. In some authorities this figure is about a half.

5.6   These figures reflect the extent of truancy, exclusion and disaffection from education, particularly among older children in care. The SSI/OFSTED inspection *The Education of Children who are Looked After* (1995) found that attendance problems for looked after children increase with age so that, at key stage 4, about 25% do not attend school regularly. Although exclusion plays a part in this, so too does falling between schools and drifting when a child moves placement. The Social Exclusion Unit report *"Truancy and School Exclusion"*, Cm 3957, May 1998. states that:

- the permanent exclusion rate among children in care *(sic)* is 10 times higher than the average

- perhaps as many as 30% of children in care are out of mainstream education, whether through exclusion or truancy.

5.7　The National Priorities Guidance target looks for an improvement in the educational achievement of looked after children. The problems of truancy, exclusion and disaffection will need to be tackled in order to achieve progress. The target is to:

Improve the educational attainment of children looked after, by increasing to at least 50% by 2001 the proportion of children leaving care at 16 or later with a GCSE or GNVQ qualification; and to 75% by 2003.

5.8　The Department believe that local councillors have an important responsibility In ensuring that sufficient priority and resources is given to this work. They should be receiving regular progress reports on how their authority is working to achieve the NPG target.

5.9　Information on the educational attainment of children looked after is currently very limited. Table 5.1 provides the best information currently available. It is taken from a pilot collection of outcome indicators for children looked after by local authorities. Although ten authorities volunteered to take part in the pilot, in the end only four local authorities were able to provide any information at all. This situation will change with the introduction of a new collection system and as a result of Quality Protects. Local authorities have been asked to set out baselines for these indicators and will have to set up the collection systems to do so.

5.10　These figures only provide a baseline. They are, of course, based on very limited data, but the number of children in the sample is quite large in comparison with some research samples. 26% of the 82 young people leaving the care of two authorities had no educational qualification. This supports the limited research evidence that formed the basis for the National Priorities Guidance target.

5.11　The information on National Curriculum Tests, traces how attainment levels appear to deteriorate as looked after children get older. Clearly if improved results are to be achieved for looked after children and children in need at GCSE/GNVQ level, social care and education attention should be directed at children's educational needs throughout their school lives. Social work assessments need to discover children whose educational attainment is suffering for social or family reasons and which can be helped by social care help.

Table 5.1 Education indicators for a sample of looked after children, 1997/98

3 local authorities in England   numbers and percentages

	All children in sample	Children in 3 local authorities			Percentage of all children in subgroup[1]
		A	B	C	
Number of children looked after continuously during 1997/98	826	259	153	414	*100*
Of these, the number of children who, during the year:					
should have sat SATS test for 7 year olds[2]	39	12	9	18	*100*
actually sat SATS test for 7 year olds[2]	29	9	9	11	*74*
achieved at least level 2 in reading, maths and science	19	8	6	5	*49*
should have sat SATS test for 11 year olds[2]	54	14	17	23	*100*
actually sat SATS test for 11 year olds[2]	40	11	14	15	*74*
achieved at least level 4 in English, maths and science	15	6	4	5	*28*
should have sat SATS test for 14 year olds[2]	56	20	10	26	*100*
actually sat SATS test for 14 year olds[2]	39	12	7	20	*70*
achieved at least level 5 in English, maths and science	4	-	1	3	*7*
were old enough to sit GCSEs	107	38	33	36	*100*
actually sat GCSEs	68	22	13	33	*64*
achieved at least 1 GCSE at grade A-G	40	19	6	15	*37*
achieved at least 5 GCSEs at grade A-C	6	3	2	1	*6*
Number of children old enough to receive full-time schooling during the school year ending July 1997	**619**	**207**	**120**	**292**	*100*
Of these, the number who, during the school year were:					
at at least SEN stage 3	160	..	55	105	*39*
at SEN stage 5	159	41	38	80	*26*
excluded from school	39	3	14	22	*6*
Number of young people leaving care during 1997/98, aged 16 or older	**82**	**60**	**22**	**..**	*100*
Of these, the number who:					
achieved at least 1 GCSE grade A-G or GNVQ	21	14	7	..	*26*
achieved at least 5 GCSEs at grade A-C	11	7	4	..	*13*

1 Where data are incomplete figures are expressed as a percentage of appropriate total
2 Now known as National Curriculum Tests
.. not available

5.12   The National Planning Guidance target is modest. The first, and very important step, is to establish the need for improvement and to set up the information systems to enable local authorities to monitor progress. The revised government objectives for children's services will introduce a broader range of performance indicators that are both more challenging and more discriminating. These indicators include attainment levels of looked after children at each key stage and the numbers attaining 5 or more GSE grades A-C by comparison with all children in the local authority. They also include the rates of permanent exclusion and the rates for children missing school *for what ever reason* for 25 days or more in a year.

Other outcome measures

5.13　Table 5.2 sets out what is known currently about outcomes other than educational attainment.

Table 5.2 Outcome indicators for a sample of looked after children, 1997/98

4 local authorities in England	All children in sample	Children in 4 local authorities[2]				Percentage of all children in sample or subgroup[1]
		A	B	C	D	
Number of children looked after continuously during 1997/98	879	259	153	414	53	*100*
Of these, the number during the year who:						
had been convicted or cautioned for an offence	24	10	14	..	..	6
attended an Accident & Emergency Unit	28	2	22	..	4	6
had an ongoing physical health condition or disability	183	59	30	94	-	*21*
had an ongoing mental health condition or disability	35	24	11	..	-	*8*
had attempted self harm or suicide	10	-	5	1	4	*1*
had their routine immunisations up to date	125	..	125	..	..	82
had not visited a dentist	19	..	19	..	..	*12*
Number of girls aged between 12 and 16	141	47	25	56	13	*100*
number of these who became pregnant during the year	3	..	2	..	1	8
number of these who gave birth during the year	1	-	1	..	-	*1*
Number under 5 years old	139	46	25	58	10	*100*
number of these with developmental reviews up to date	22	..	22	..	..	88
number recorded as developmentally delayed	13	..	5	8	..	*16*
Number aged 16 years old or older	210	70	29	108	3	*100*
Of these the number at 31 March 1998 who were						
unemployed	36	22	13	..	1	35
employed	13	7	6	..	-	*13*
in education or training	64	41	21	..	2	63

1 Where data are incomplete figures are expressed as a percentage of appropriate total

2 The figures for authority D are for one area office

.. not available

5.14   These outcome measures are less easy to obtain than educational attainment due to the small numbers of children involved in these estimates and must therefore be treated with caution. They are presented here to illustrate what it is intended to provide in the future, and highlights the important measures of the success of corporate parenting under the Children Act.

5.15   One or two of these indicators have been dropped from the full-scale collection - notably figures for pregnancy and births, because the numbers are too small to be used for comparative purposes.

5.16   The government objectives now due include a performance indicator based on the proportion of children looked after who have had the required routine immunisations: who had their teeth checked and who had an annual health assessment. Also, there is an indicator based on the proportion of children looked after aged 10 years or over who have been cautioned or convicted of an offence, compared with, the proportion for all children aged 10 years or over who have been cautioned or convicted.

5.17   Finally, there is an indicator based on the proportion of children looked after from ethnic minorities compared with the proportion of children from ethnic minorities in the local authority area.

New collections of outcomes for looked after children

5.18   Two national statistical collections have been introduced to monitor outcome and performance indicators for looked after children as described above.

5.19   The first collection deals with the educational attainment of care leavers and will enable the Departments of Health and Education and Employment to assess progress towards the national target for educational attainment of these children. Local authorities will provide a summary of the educational qualifications of every young person leaving their care aged 16 years or older each year.

5.20   The second collection covers a range of outcome indicators for children who have been looked after continuously for a year. Authorities will provide information about:

• National Curriculum Tests

• GCSE results

• school attendance and exclusion

• offending

• immunisation, medical and dental checks, and

• employment and training.

5.21 The Department believes that local councillors have an important role as corporate parents and that they should receive information on the indicators and outcome measures suggested above on how well the children for whom they have a parental responsibility are doings.

5.22 This is a key task in the Quality Protects programme and must command urgent attention.

Messages from Inspection

Someone Else's Children: The Inspections of Planning and Decision Making for Children Looked After and the Safety of Children Looked After (1998) found:

- Health care was usually addressed in children's care plans but often in a fairly perfunctory way. There were particular problems in meeting the health needs of children with severe behavioural and/or psychiatric problems

- the same was true in relation to education. There were high levels of school exclusion of looked after children particularly those in residential care

- as with psychiatric care needs of these children, SSDs were having to shoulder an unfair burden in making up shortfalls elsewhere in the system.

Voluntary Children's Homes

SSI inspections of voluntary children's homes (VCHs) are both an ongoing source of information about what the experiences of some looked after children are, and are a regular window on the activity of voluntary organisations. Observations drawn from inspections indicate that:

- VCHs also experience problems with children being excluded from school, particularly those of secondary school age. Some VCHs have created specialist posts to support children's education using voluntary funds. Others are providing education for children who are not attending school

- those VCHs who accept referrals from local authorities other than the one in which they are situated sometimes experience considerable difficulty in obtaining specialist education placements for children with statements of special educational need

- VCHs also struggle with health and behaviour problems. Some VCHs are appointing health specialists

- VCHs who have a clearly defined statement of purpose and function and are clear about the children that they work with most successfully, do appear to achieve better outcomes for children. This is primarily marked by less frequent breakdowns in placement and children moving on in a positive and planned manner

- VCHs are, however, increasingly subject to market forces and have occupancy targets to meet and those in contracts with local authorities can come under pressure to define the statements of purpose and function broadly in order to give the local authority maximum flexibility about who they place in the VCH

- whilst clear background information is often a contractual requirement prior to placement, they may not insist on this before accepting a referral. Where information is not shared prior to placement this can result in inappropriate placement

- written care plans are often poor. Looked After Children forms are increasingly being used but are often not properly completed. Full use is not made of the assessment and action records and there is little evidence of assessments being carried out prior to a placement being made

- reviews are normally held within the prescribed timescales, but the minutes are often not made available to the home for weeks after the event, affecting planning for children

- VCHs are often working with some of the most damaged children in the public care and struggle in the absence of clear care plans and background information

- where the child does not have an allocated social worker, or where there are frequent changes of social workers, planning for the child suffers

- some VCHs act as very effective advocates for children and become involved in aspects of the child's life outside the home, arranging contact with significant people and where necessary supervising this contact

- some children remain in contact with the home long after they have left, with staff providing informal support and a point of contact.

Life Chances of Care Leavers

Objective: To ensure that young people leaving care, as they enter adulthood, are not isolated and participate socially and economically as citizens.

Introduction

6.1   This chapter concerns children who at the age of about 16 years are being looked after and are entering 'adulthood' heavily dependent upon the support they receive from the local authority. It is known that the future of these children is precarious.

6.2   The objective is intended to ensure that young people are not encouraged to leave care prematurely and that they are given help at this critical stage of transition.

6.3   Section 24 of the Children Act requires local authorities to advise, assist and befriend each looked after child with a view to protecting his or her welfare after (s)he ceases to be looked after. They also have a duty to advise and befriend young people they have looked after beyond their 16th birthday, until they are 21, but they only have a power, not a duty, to assist them in kind or, exceptionally, in cash.

6.4   "In response to the Children's Safeguards Review, the Government has said that it will legislate to replace the current discretionary power to assist with a duty to assess and meet the needs of care leavers up to age 18. Consideration will be given to extending this up to the age of 21. Other measures to be introduced will include giving local authorities the power to assist with the costs of education and training up to the age of 24. New arrangements are proposed for 16 and 17 year olds living in and leaving care with the aim of ensuring that young people only leave care when they are ready to do so and also to improve their life chances. The new arrangements, as set out in the consultation paper "Me, Survive, Out There?", will place responsibility on local authorities to provide personal and financial support for these young people; to draw up individual pathway plans for their transition to adulthood; and to appoint a personal adviser for each young person."

The number of care leavers

6.5   During the year ending 31 March 1998, 7,800 young people left the care of local authorities in England, aged 16 years or older. As can be seen in Figure 6.1:

- half of these had been looked after for 2 or more years

- but a quarter had been looked after for less than 6 months

- many had been in foster placements (47%)

- 23% were living in children's homes and

- 17% were already in lodgings or living independently.

Figure 6.1 Children aged 16 and over who ceased to be looked after during the year ending 31 March 1998, by duration of final period of care, and by final placement

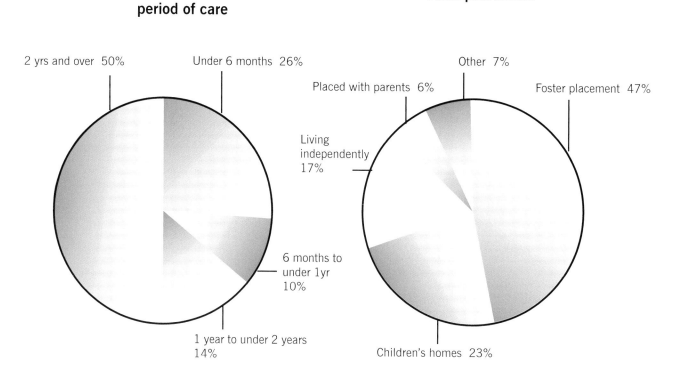

Duration of final period of care

Final placement

7,800 care leavers, aged 16 and over, 1997/98

Table 6.1 Children aged 15 and over who ceased to be looked after during the years ending 31 March 1994 to 1998[1]

England   numbers and percentages

	numbers					percentages				
	1994	1995	1996	1997	1998	1994	1995	1996	1997	1998
Age on ceasing										
15	2,800	3,200	3,300	3,100	2,900	24	27	28	27	28
16	3,000	3,400	3,500	3,400	3,600	26	28	30	30	33
17	1,500	1,400	1,500	1,500	1,400	13	12	12	13	13
18 birthday	4,300	3,900	3,500	3,300	2,700	36	32	29	29	25
Older than 18th Birthday	180	160	100	100	130	1	1	1	1	1
All children[2]	**11,800**	**12,100**	**12,000**	**11,400**	**10,700**	**100**	**100**	**100**	**100**	**100**
Final legal status										
Care Orders										
15	180	180	150	160	140	5	6	6	7	6
16	220	200	190	160	200	6	7	7	7	9
17	220	160	160	150	230	7	6	6	6	11
18th birthday	2,700	2,300	2,100	1,900	1,500	79	79	80	80	70
Older than 18th Birthday	90	50	10	10	70	3	2	1	-	4
All children[2]	3,400	2,900	2,600	2,400	2,100	100	100	100	100	100
Voluntary agreements (S20)										
15	**2,200**	**2,600**	**2,700**	**2,400**	**2,300**	31	33	34	32	33
16	2,200	2,600	2,700	2,500	2,600	31	33	34	33	37
17	1,100	1,100	1,200	1,200	1,100	15	14	14	16	15
18th birthday	1,600	1,500	1,400	1,400	1,100	22	19	17	18	15
Older than 18th Birthday	80	100	80	90	60	1	1	1	1	1
All children[2]	7,200	7,800	8,100	7,600	7,100	100	100	100	100	100
Other										
15	400	470	430	470	450	33	35	34	34	32
16	600	610	620	700	820	50	46	49	51	57
17	160	160	140	140	100	13	12	12	10	7
18th birthday	50	90	70	70	60	4	7	5	5	4
Older than 18th Birthday	-	-	-	-	-	-	-	-	-	-
All children[2]	1,200	1,300	1,300	1,400	1,400	100	100	100	100	100

1 Only the latest occassion on which a child ceased to be looked after in the year has been counted

2 Figures for children looked after in this table exclude agreed series of short term placements

Figure 6.2 Number of children aged 15 & 16 ceasing to be looked after by week of age after 15th birthday 1992/93 to 1997/98

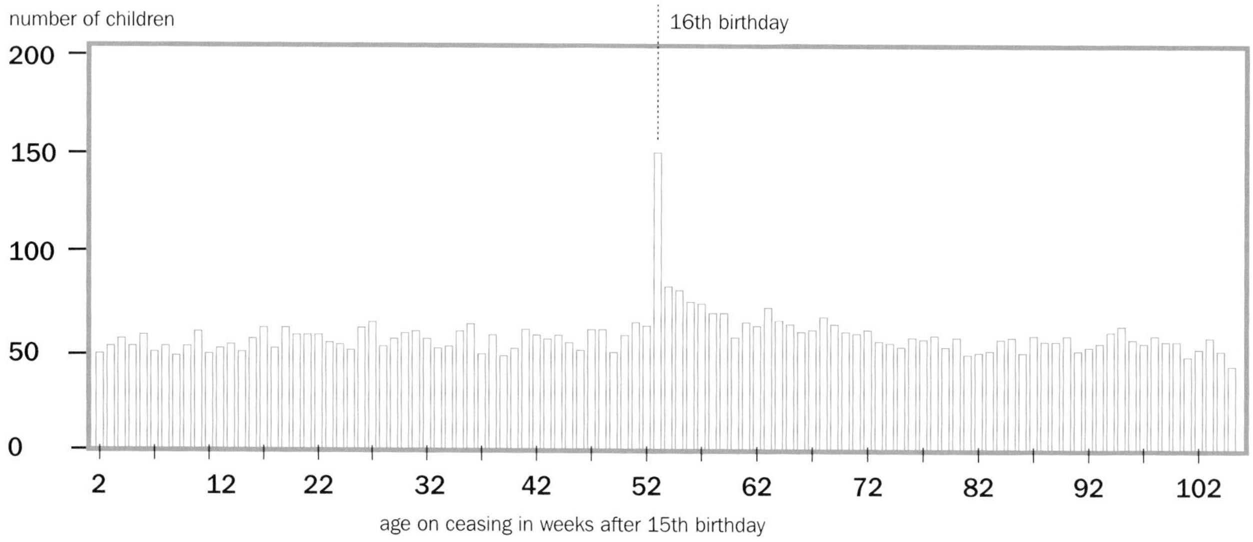

The age at which children move on from being looked after

6.6   Table 6.1 shows figures for the numbers of children leaving care aged 15 or over, by age and by legal status. The overall number of young people leaving care in this age group has fallen since 1995. The biggest fall has been in the number and proportion leaving care on their 18th birthday, many of whom were under care orders. In contrast, the proportion leaving care aged 16 has risen. This rise was particularly marked between 1997 and 1998 across all legal status categories, and provides a preliminary indication that some young people who previously would have been looked after until they reached 18 are now leaving care at the age of 16.

6.7   Figure 6.2 provides a different perspective. This shows the number of 15 and 16-year-olds leaving care by age in weeks. There is a clear peak in the week of the 16th birthday and in subsequent weeks, and this trend has been growing in recent years.

6.8   It is not clear whether these figures reflect a desire by authorities to discharge children soon after their 16th birthday, or the pressure from the young people themselves to be independent as soon as they turn 16 years. The Department of Health will continue to use statistics to monitor the trend.

Support for care leavers

6.9 The increasing trend to discharge young people early from "voluntary care" may reflect cost saving measures by authorities. However, the majority of families continue to support their children at least until the age of 18 years and care leavers are likely to be more dependent than others at that age in view of the personal difficulties they have experienced.

6.10 How well looked after young people do as they enter adulthood represents the culmination of their experience throughout childhood. If they move towards independent adulthood without the ongoing help and support that other young people can expect from their families, they are at a great disadvantage. If good work has been put into the care and support of young people up to the age of 16 years, consigning them to premature independence, is likely, simply, to throw away the investment.

6.11 There are, therefore, very good reasons for focusing attention on care leavers and increasing the resources directed at their needs. There are a number of initiatives being pursued to this end. Special grant money is available through the Quality Protects programme to improve and extent leaving care schemes.

The National Priorities Guidance Target

6.12 Progress will be made towards this objective of improving life chances only if local authorities find effective ways of maintaining contact and supporting young people who they are looking after when they turn 16. The need for local authorities to support young people for longer and be more pro-active in assisting them into a productive adulthood is expressed in the National Priorities Guidance target to:

Demonstrate that the level of employment, training or education amongst young people aged 19 in 2001/02 who were looked after by Local Authorities in their 17th year on 1 April 1999, is at least 60% of the level amongst all young people of the same age in their area.

6.13 A new statistical collection is to be established to follow up the position of care leavers on their 19th birthday. This will provide the data needed to measure the success of the national target. Local authorities will be asked to provide details about the 16 year olds they were looking after on 1 April 1999 and each April thereafter once they reach 19 years old. Authorities will provide information about where each young person is living and about whether they are in education, training or employment.

6.14   Local authorities are asked to compare the outcomes for care leavers with the local outcomes for young people generally. At a national level the Careers Service publish information about the numbers of young people engaged in education training or employment (activity status). Table 6.2 summarises this information for 16 year olds.

Table 6.2 Activity Status in Autumn 1998 of young people completing Year 11 in 1998

England		numbers and percentages
	numbers of young people completing Year 11 in 1998	percentages of young people completing Year 11 in 1998
All young people	**553,736**	*100*
Full time education	378,818	*68.4*
Government supported training:	48,512	*8.8*
– training scheme funded by the Goverment	32,242	*5.8*
– job, including training which is supported by Government funding	16,270	*2.9*
Employment outside Government supported training:	50,020	*9.0*
– job, including planned training which is not supported by Government funding	26,679	*4.8*
– job without planned training	23,341	*4.2*
Not settled:	40,116	*7.2*
– not active in the labour market	6,996	*1.3*
– economically active but not in full time education, training or employment	33,120	*5.9*
Moved out of contact of Careers Service	12,825	*2.3*
No response to follow-up	23,445	*4.2*

Source: Moving On 1998 – Pathways taken by Young People beyond 16 : the Careers Service Activity Survey, DfEE (1999)

Messages from Inspection

When leaving care is leaving home: The Inspection of Leaving Care Services (1997) found:

- some SSDs assumed that to be prepared for leaving statutory care meant changing placement to live in specialist resources. This made foster carers wary of services from leaving care teams

- that even if living with their family or friends, the level of support needed is as great as being in care. Those in supported schemes got excellent support and appreciated it

- there were few opportunities for education and social care and there were missed opportunities relating to health needs. Where there were facilities for information and advice this was welcomed

- there were considerable variations in psychology and psychiatry services available to SSDs

- SSDs had difficulty getting useful agreements with other agencies. Good examples of housing and education schemes tended to be where there was a sympathetic senior manager in the other agency

- too often staff were satisfied if the young person had accommodation and was signing on. Where a team had responsibility for the 16 + year olds they were better able to negotiate schemes and individual packages

- SSDs did not have tracking systems for their care leavers. Where an effort was made in a friendly way to keep in touch, young people were more likely to ask for help when they needed it

- in some SSDs young people had to refer themselves as new cases if they had lost touch

- some SSDs had provided very positive support for counselling for 21 + years, who were able to benefit and understand the reasons they were looked after.

Services for Disabled Children and their Families

Objective: To ensure that children with specific social needs arising out of disability [or a health need] are living in families or other appropriate settings in the community where their assessed needs are adequately met and reviewed.

Introduction

7.1 The Children Act and subsequent guidance provides the framework for local authorities in relation to services for disabled children. They should be based on the following principles:

- the welfare of the child should be safeguarded and promoted

- disabled children are children first

- the views of children should be sought and taken into account

- recognition of the importance of parents and families in children's lives

- partnership between parents and agency staff

- the race, culture, religion and language of the child and family should be taken into account when providing services

- a primary aim should be to promote the access for all children to the same range of services

- assessment and planning for and provision of services should be led by the social services department but undertaken in partnership with other statutory and voluntary agencies.

Information about disability

7.2 Information about disabled children is outdated. There is no authoritative national information about services received by disabled children and their families. The best source of information is from two surveys carried out by OPCS (now the Office of National Statistics) more than a decade ago, and, therefore, pre-dates the Children Act. These were a survey of households in 1985 and a survey of communal living establishments in 1988 – see Tables 7.1. Further, more detailed, analysis of the OPCS data has been undertaken in recent years. Some limited data is also available from returns on local authority disability registers. It is the Department's intention to remedy this situation.

The OPCS Surveys

7.3 The OPCS surveys found that:

- 360,000 children (under 16 years) had disabilities in Great Britain. This represented a rate of 32 per 1,000

- over 90% lived with their parents

- 5,600 were in communal living establishments

- those in establishments tended to have severest disabilities but even so only 4% of all children with the severest disabilities were cared for in establishments

- children in residential establishments had on average 3.3 disabilities compared with 2.6 for those living in families

- relatively more boys than girls had disabilities.

Table 7.1 Estimates of numbers of disabled children in Great Britain by severity of disability, 1985

Great Britain   numbers

Severity   numbers of disabled children

	Total	In private households	In communal establishments[1]
All catergories	**360,000**	**355,000**	**5,600**
1	33,000	33,000	100
2	19,000	18,000	100
3	48,000	48,000	500
4	43,000	42,000	500
5	43,000	42,000	1,000
6	38,000	37,000	600
7	46,000	45,000	700
8	31,000	31,000	300
9	25,000	25,000	400
10(most severe)	34,000	33,000	1,500

1 Figures are for 1988

Table 7.2 Prevelence of disability among children in Great Britain by age and sex, rates per thousand population, 1985				
Great Britain		rates per thousand population in age group		
	All ages	Age group		
		0 - 4	5 – 9	10 - 15
All disabled children	32	21	38	35
Boys	37	24	45	42
Girls	26	18	30	29

7.4   Smaller studies containing later data indicate that the population is broadly similar but there appear to be significant increases in the number of younger children with complex medical needs, and of older children who are diagnosed as having autism type disorders and Hyperactivity Disorder Attention Deficit (ADHD).

7.5   Two important aspects of the OPCS work should be noted. Firstly, impairments that do not lead to disabilities were not included. Secondly, behavioural and emotional difficulties were treated as disabilities, whether or not they were associated with any specific psychiatric or organic disorder.

Further analysis of the OPCS surveys

7.6   Gordon, Parker and Loughram undertook further analysis of the OPCS data in 1992 and 1996 *(Children with Disabilities in Communal Establishments: a further analysis of the OPCS Investigation and Children with Disabilities in Private Households: a re-analysis of the OPCS investigation.* The 1998 publication is *Disabled Children: Directions for Their Future Care (SSI).* They derived estimates for the numbers of looked after Children with disabilities. They estimate that in England and Wales:

- about a quarter of looked after children have disabilities compared with about 3.2% of under 18s as a whole. Disabled children, therefore, have a greater likelihood of being 'looked after'

- 86% of disabled children living in communal establishments are looked after although the children with severest conditions tend to be in NHS care.

7.7   These figures represent the statistical background to the provisions of Sections 85 and 86 of the Act which require that children, not looked after but placed away from home for more than three months, are notified to the Local Authority. The Authority must then consider whether action is needed to safeguard and promote the child's welfare.

7.8   Gordon *et al* examined socio-economic characteristics, family composition
        and disability and drew attention to the greater likelihood of disabled children
        coming from disadvantaged backgrounds:

- 55% of households with children with disabilities were living in poverty,
  or on its margins, in 1985

- yet families with the lowest 20% of incomes received fewer services than
  all other families.

**Table 7.3 Percentage of children with disabilities and children in households
classified by socio-economic group of head household, 1985**

Great Britain   percentages and ratios

Socio-economic group	Disabled children (1985 OPCS Disability Survey)	All children in households(1985 General Household Survey)	Ratio of percentage of disabled children to percentage of all children
All households	*100*	*100*	1
Professionals	*4.5*	*7.2*	0.63
Employers and Managers	*15.5*	*20.1*	0.77
Intermediate Non-Manual	*7.6*	*8.9*	0.85
Junior Non-Manual	*7.9*	*8.2*	0.96
Skilled Manual	*37.6*	*35.9*	1.04
Semi-skilled Manual	*19.2*	*15.9*	1.21
Unskilled Manual	*7.7*	*3.8*	2.03

7.9   Lone parents and large families were found to fare significantly worse than
        others in terms of receiving services. So, surprisingly, whereas 1 in 10 of the
        families containing two adults and a single child had had respite care, the
        ratio fell to 1 in 50 amongst families where there were two adults and 4 or
        more children, and to 1 in 20 amongst lone parents.

Other sources of information

7.10   A survey conducted in 1996 MORI/York NCB Survey of Children in Need
        (1996) estimated that 44,000 children in England were identified by social
        services departments as receiving services because they were disabled. This
        is equivalent to about 11% of all children in need but no breakdown by
        disabling conditions was given. There would have been differences between
        local authorities in how they defined "disability" and the estimate is based on
        grossing up from a sample which will carry some error, so these figures must
        be treated only as a broad indicator.

7.11   This estimate suggests that the proportion of disabled children receiving services from local authorities at any one time is small compared with all disabled children. The numbers of disabled children receiving support in the course of a year will, however, be larger and many families will be receiving support through health services, schools and voluntary organisations.

The need for improved information

7.12   Both *People Like Us* and *The Second Report of the Health Select Committee on Children Looked After by Local Authorities* expressed concern about the inadequacy of the existing information base and recommended that reliable statistics should be obtained. Because most disabled children known to social services have a multiplicity of disabilities, it is by no means straight forward deciding how best to capture their needs and circumstances statistically. The Department is considering how this might best be done and further information will be included in subsequent reports. Discussion will be needed with those with responsibility for health and education services since it would be helpful to use common, or at least compatible, definitions.

7.13   The Children in Need Data Collection currently being introduced across all authorities will, once fully established, provide an annual broad picture of the numbers of children with illness or disability receiving services from social services departments, along with information on the type of service response and related expenditure.

Messages from Inspection

- numerous positive instances that the majority of agencies and individuals were working towards services being provided in partnership with families and other agencies in line with the values and principles which underlie the Children Act

- authorities were not planning on the basis of a thorough analysis of need

- only a few health authorities were undertaking local need assessments based on sound epidemiological evidence

- due to legislative requirements, local education authorities had comprehensive data bases for children with Special Educational Needs but the information was not generally shared with other agencies

- considerable progress had been made in setting up registers of disabled children but links between registers and planning mechanisms were poorly developed.

The Quality Protects objectives and disabled children

7.14　Clearly any child with a disability or a health need should benefit from all the relevant Quality Protects objectives. They should:

- be firmly attached to carers

- be protected from abuse

- have their needs fully assessed with action plans and reviewed

- have maximum life chances and

- be helped in the transition to adulthood.

7.15　Many disabled children will have additional needs for services, for example high levels of personal care or physical adaptations to the places in which they live. There are, therefore, separate objectives and sub-objectives to cover the specific needs of disabled children

7.16　Local authorities are required to arrive at a complete picture of the population of disabled children in their areas and to provide an increasing level of service for disabled children both through short term breaks and home based support.

Messages from Inspection

Some of the findings from inspection reports are relevant to particular Quality Protects objectives. The following points are from ***Removing Barriers for Disabled Children: The Inspection of Services to Disabled Children*** (1998) and, in the case of Objective 5, ***When Leaving Home is Leaving Care: The Inspection of Leaving Care Services*** (1997):

Objective 1 Secure attachment. Planned short term arrangements

- services were determined in partnership with parents, and, to a lesser extent. with disabled children

- for some parents dealing with service providers was very stressful. For some it was the most difficult aspect of caring for their children

- parents saw respite care as critical. Provision was variable but it was qenerally a planned predictable service for families

Objective 2 Protection against abuse

- the child's welfare was not always central to the practice of workers

- specialist workers were often ill informed about child protection issues. However, there was some good inter-agency training in child protection and disabled children

Objective 3 Maximising life chance benefits

- there were limited opportunities for disabled children to make choices about their lifestyles and the services available to them

- agencies accepted there was a decline in collaborative work when the child was aged 5 +

- in most authorities continuing care services for children had not been satisfactorily resolved.

Objective 5 Leaving Care

- more emphasis was needed on children's rights and empowerment rather than on parents' wishes.

- reviews needed to be improved and young people included in them, and to cover living, social and developmental needs as well as education and health information.

Objective 6 Disabled Children

- many disabled children and their families said that the services they received were of good quality, but were not always timely or flexible

- senior managers acknowledged that progress in joint planning and commissioning of services for disabled children and their families had been limited.

Objective 7 Assessment and Decision Making

- access to services was often difficult and there were waiting lists for assessments

- a frequent complaint from service users was the continual opening and closing of cases.

Objective 8 Resource Planning

- demand for services was high in all authorities, and provision was still predominantly service-led

- there was little systematic monitoring of customer satisfaction

- concentration on eligibility for services and not on meeting needs, led to more expensive care being offered rather than cheaper services which took time to set up

- most agencies had not set measurable objectives and outcomes and could not, therefore, effectively review performance

- there were excellent examples of gaining and evaluating the views of disabled children and their families about services but ways of feeding this into the planned systems were under-developed.

Policy Development

7.17   There are now unparalleled opportunities for turning aspirations for co-ordinated multi-agency services for disabled children into reality. Joint planning of services across agency boundaries should help disabled children and their families who have persistently reported fragmentation and inconsistency between services. In November 1998 DfEE published *Meeting Special Educational Needs*, a programme of action which sets out what needs to be done to realise the Government's vision for children with special needs, many of whom will be disabled. Inclusion and multi-agency working are key themes of DfEE policy which are replicated in current DH priorities. The powers in the Health Services Act for pooled budgets and other organisational flexibilities are likely to be particularly relevant to services for disabled children. The message for joint planning has been delivered to the major providing agencies for disabled children:

- to Health in the Health Improvement Programmes and Joint Investment Plans

- to Education in the Early Years Development Plans and Behaviour Support Plans and

- to Social Services in the Children's Services Plans and Quality Protects Management Action Plans.

7.18   Each plan must link together just as each service for disabled children should link together. Voluntary organisations and parents groups are key to the success of joint planning bringing a user perspective to ensure that the entire exercise is focused on the needs of the disabled child.

Assessment and Decision Making

Objective: To ensure that referral and assessment processes discriminate effectively between different types and levels of need and produce timely service responses.

Introduction

8.1   The Children Act 1989 lays a duty on every local authority:

- to safeguard and promote the welfare of children within their area who are in need; and

- so far as is consistent with that duty, to promote the upbringing of such children by their families, by providing a range and level of services appropriate to those children's needs (Section17(1)).

8.2   As explained in Chapter 4, the Children Act defines "children in need" as children "unlikely to achieve or maintain ... a reasonable standard of health and development" without services; whose health and development will be significantly impaired without services; or who are disabled (Section 17 (10)). Applying this definition in practice has not proved easy for social service departments. In order to find out whether a child is in need, careful assessment is required in which all the relevant information has been analysed and recorded as the basis for professional judgement, planning and action.

8.3   Where there are concerns about a child's welfare because of suspicions that a child "is suffering, or is likely to suffer, significant harm", Section 47 of the Children Act requires the local authority to make enquiries to "enable them to decide whether they should take any action to safeguard and promote the child's welfare". Government guidance *Working Together Under the Children Act 1989* (now revised) set out the arrangements to be put in place by all agencies to ensure the protection of children from abuse. It builds on the Children Act and sets down a timescale - eight working days – within which initial child protection conferences should normally be convened from the date of referral unless there are particular reasons for the delay.

8.4   There is currently no statistical information at national level on performance with respect to this objective. This Chapter sets out current developments and information from inspections.

Findings from Inspection and Research

8.5   SSI inspections and research commissioned by the Department of Health (*Child Protection: Messages from Research* 1995) have found that a substantial proportion of social services departments and other agency resources were being directed into assessment. This did not necessarily mean children and their families received help or, if they did, the sort of help they would benefit from. Assessments undertaken where there were child protection concerns tended to focus on whether or not an incident of abuse had taken place, rather than looking at the child's needs within a child development and family context. The best practitioners used the findings of their assessment to inform their child care plans and subsequent interventions, but this was not universally so. The timescales set out in *'Working Together Under the Children Act 1989'* presented a challenge in many social service departments and were considered to allow insufficient time to undertake an initial assessment prior to the child protection conference. Many comprehensive assessments took several months to complete and in some inspections there was evidence of them not being completed.

8.6   *Child Protection: Messages from Research 1995* and inspection work highlighted the importance of assessments taking account of parents' situations and considering what help they might need to enable them to safeguard and promote their children's development. In particular, parents were found to be experiencing problems of domestic violence, problem alcohol and drug use and mental illness and poverty. In social services departments there has been increasing concern about how to ensure assessments are carried out in a manner that identifies the child's needs and results in appropriate help being given to the child and family, but which neither intervenes too intrusively nor too little.

Messages from Inspection

Getting Family Support Right: The Inspection of the Delivery of Family Support Services (1999) found:

- practitioners were skilled at working in partnership with parents

- new formats for undertaking assessment were being developed in some authorities

- joint planning with other agencies in complex family support cases was becoming more commonplace but there was uncertainty about which cases this should apply to

- family centres and half the Child and Mental Health social work services were systematically reviewing their work, often against stated objectives

- however, thinking by practitioners about outcomes in the work was only in its infancy

---

Assessing children to safeguard and promote their welfare

8.7   New time-scales for undertaking assessments have been set out in the Government's objectives for children's social services. There is an expectation that a decision will be made within 24 hours on what response is required to a referral or new information on an open case. The sub-objectives also set out maximum limits for undertaking initial and core assessments. They have been agreed at 7 and 35 working days respectively after the date of the referral (or following the receipt of new information) to a social services department. Within these timescales, there is an expectation that initial child protection conferences will be held a maximum of 15 working days from the date of the strategy discussion at which the decision is made to initiate a Section 47 enquiry. Specialist assessments commissioned by social service departments may take longer to complete and are not included in these time-scales.

8.8   The Department of Health has developed a new framework for assessing the needs of children and their families which will provide the foundation for future action by social service departments to safeguard and promote children's welfare (Department of Health 1999). Any assessment of a child and his or her family will take account of:

- the child's developmental needs

- the parenting capacity of the child's carers to respond to these needs

- relevant wider family and environmental factors.

8.9   These three domains interact and have a direct impact on the current well-being of a child and the achievement of longer term optimal outcomes. They constitute a framework for assessment and an understanding of what is happening to a child.

8.10   Findings from the assessment will enable staff assessing a child to identify whether a child's health and development are being or are likely to be impaired by their present circumstances and provide evidence about whether a child is a child in need according to Section 17 of the Children Act. A continuing concern for child welfare agencies must be whether the harm or impairment a child is experiencing is significant. The new assessment framework, which builds on the child development dimensions in the Looking After Children system, will be embedded in the new *Working Together to Safeguard Children*. Thus, for the first time children who are referred to a social services department will be assessed according to the same dimensions irrespective of their presenting needs.

8.11   A social services department, in collaboration with other agencies, will use the framework to underpin policy, practice and systems within which assessments of children and families are carried out. The intention is for staff to apply the framework from the first point of contact, through initial and core assessments and at a depth, which has been determined by the child's needs. The provision of appropriate services should not await the end of the assessment but be offered when they are required by the child and family. This is likely to be at points throughout the assessment. The process of engaging in an assessment should be therapeutic and conceived of as part of the range of services offered.

8.12 The new assessment framework will emphasise the use of evidence when making judgements about children's welfare and deciding whether, and how best, to provide services for children and families. This evidence will relate to the child's developmental progress, parents capacity to respond appropriately to identified needs and the wider family and environmental context in which the child is growing up.

Messages from Inspection

Someone Else's Children: The Inspections of Planning and Decision Making for Children Looked After and The Safety of Children Looked After (1998) found:

- social workers did a great deal of fact gathering but were less good at structuring it and drawing conclusions from it

- it was often difficult to discern how decisions were reached on the basis of the information recorded. Decision making needed to be more explicit. Plans should flow logically from the assessment

- social workers were beginning to see assessment as a separate task to be specially commissioned outside of the normal social worker's job

Resource Planning

Objective: To ensure that resources are planned and provided at levels which represent best value for money, allow for choice and different responses for different needs and circumstances.

Introduction

9.1 This objective requires local authorities, in conjunction with other agencies concerned with children, to examine:

- how they respond to needs for personal social services, and

- how public money is spent in responding and

- the outputs and outcomes achieved.

9.2 This is complex and difficult. There are many ways in which need and outcomes are influenced by factors some of which are beyond a department's control. It is necessary to try to understand the relationship between:

- the inputs to personal social services for children

- the service outputs

- and outcomes for children.

9.3 In order to do this, the various influences have to be identified, explained and measured. Having done so there may still be further variation, which requires explanation .

9.4 This Chapter explores some of the factors which explain how local authorities respond to need and the variations between them. It looks at:

- patterns of expenditure

- the supply side

- the underlying needs and demands

Patterns of expenditure

9.5 In 1997 £2.2 billion was spent on children's personal social services. Over a number of years this has varied as set out in Table 9.1. These figures and those in Table 9.2 include all expenditure which can be related to children's services, including overhead costs. In the other figures in this Chapter expenditure is broken down in more detail but, because of difficulty in apportionment, overheads are excluded.

Table 9.1 Gross annual expenditure on children's personal social services

England								£s millions
	1990-91	1991-92	1992-93	1993-94	1994-95	1995-96	1996-97	1997-98
Gross expenditure on children's personal social services								
Cash terms	936	1,021	1,099	1,156	1,931	2,033	2,142	2,256
Real terms[1]	1,162	1,193	1,244	1,274	2,099	2,147	2,195	2,256

1 Real terms: expenditure has been deflated using GDP price index, 1997-98 = 100

Note: expenditure includes cost of overheads

: The GDP price index removes the effects of inflation and thereby presents the costs in real terms.

9.6 Table 9.1 shows the increase in the total expenditure on children's personal social services. The top line takes no account of inflation. The figures in the "real terms " line are expenditure expressed in terms of the value of the pound in 1997-98. These figures take no account of the changing population size of children.

9.7 The table shows a steep rise in the figures between 1993-94 and 1994-95. This discontinuity in the data and is an artefact due to changes in the collection of this information.

9.8 Table 9.2 takes account of changes in population size by expressing expenditure per child in the population.

Table 9.2 Gross annual expenditure on children's personal services per population under 18 years

England								£s per child in population
	1990-91	1991-92	1992-93	1993-94	1994-95	1995-96	1996-97	1997-98
Gross annual expenditure on children's personal social services per population under 18 years								
Cash terms	86	94	100	105	174	182	190	200
Real terms[1]	107	109	114	116	189	192	195	200

1 Real terms: expenditure has been deflated using GDP price index, 1997-98 = 100

Note: expenditure includes cost of overheads

GDP price index – see note at Table 9.1

9.9 It is useful to try to split this overall expenditure between looked after children and other children receiving services, mainly in their families. Until more detailed information is available from the forthcoming collection of expenditure on children in need, it is necessary to split large scale expenditure using a convention. This has to be based on assumptions about how general costs are apportioned between these two types of service. The figures which follow include within expenditure on looked after children:

- residential provision
- foster care placements
- children looked after in community placements
- the guardian ad litem service
- one half of expenditure for children who have left care.

9.10   Expenditure on children not looked after includes everything else.

9.11   Overhead, field social work, occupational therapists, assistant director and
        care managers' expenditure are added in proportion to the above separation
        of expenditure. It is acknowledged that, in the absence of a recognised
        convention, these assumptions are arguable. However they do allow us to
        trace how expenditure on children looked after and children supported in
        their families or independently have varied relative to each other over a
        period of time.

9.12   Figure 9.1 shows that over a number of years up to the early 1990s the
        proportion of expenditure on children supported in their families has
        increased. This reflects the fall in the number of looked after children
        although the fall in expenditure on looked after children has not been as
        steep as the fall in their numbers largely because the cost of residential
        provision has inflated considerably as the sector has shrunk. This figure
        suggests that the implementation of the Children Act has not noticeably
        contributed to a greater proportion of expenditure on family support.

Figure 9.1 Expenditure on children looked after and children not looked after as a
percentage of gross annual expenditure on children's social services, England, years
ending 31 March 1984 to 1998

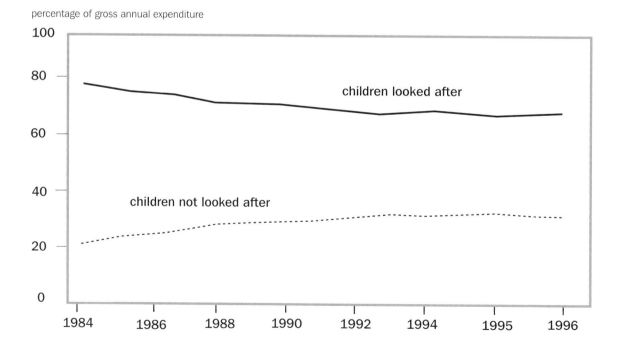

percentage of gross annual expenditure

9.13   The fall in the number of children looked after reached its low point in 1994 and has since increased by 8%. This trend would drive expenditure up and indeed there are signs that this is happening. It is known, however, that most of the increase in looked after children has been absorbed by placement in foster care which should mean that expenditure will increase by less than if the occupancy of residential care enlarged. Nonetheless this is a significant pressure on children's social care budgets.

Expenditure on looked after children

9.14   The Health Select Committee Second Report on *Children Looked After by Local Authorities* (1998) sought, in its recommendation 2, information on "the average cost to the public purse of caring for looked after children". The following information responds to this requirement drawing on financial information supplied annually to the DETR by local authorities. These figures include only those costs which can be related directly to the provision of care and accommodation for looked after children. They ***exclude*** overhead costs.

9.15   The information can be represented in several ways.

Table 9.3 Expenditure on children looked after by local authorities in England

England						£s millions, £s per week, £s per child in population		
	1990-91	1991-92	1992-93	1993-94	1994-95	1995-96	1996-97	1997-98
Gross annual expenditure on children looked after (£ millions)								
Cash terms	633	673	708	738	802	839	914	969
Real terms[1]	785	786	801	814	871	886	937	969
Gross weekly expenditure per child looked after (£'s)								
Cash terms	203	237	269	288	309	317	341	347
Real terms[1]	252	278	304	317	336	335	349	347
Gross annual expenditure on children looked after per population aged under 18 (£'s)								
Cash terms	58	62	65	67	72	75	81	86
Real terms[1]	72	72	74	74	78	79	83	86

1 Real terms: expenditure has been deflated using GDP price index, 1997-98 = 100

Note: expenditure includes cost of overheads
      GDP price index – see note at Table 9.1

9.16   Table 9.3 gives the total costs of services ascribed by local authorities to looked after children, and the unit weekly cost of the services for looking after children - covering the costs in residential care, foster care and other situations. Table 9.3 also relates public expenditure on looked after children to the total population of children. This makes allowances for variations in expenditure arising out of population changes and is the clearest way of demonstrating the real increase in expenditure. The weekly expenditure per child looked after shows nearly a 40% increase in real expenditure from 1991 to 1998.

9.17   Table 9.4 splits weekly expenditure on children in foster care from residential care. It is well known that the costs of residential care have increased at a rate significantly greater than inflation. As the sector has declined and homes have become smaller, economies of scale have been lost and unit costs have increased. In addition, research shows that, although foster carers cope with children with very complex difficulties, children's homes tend to accommodate children whose behaviour present staff with problems of control. This has tended to increase staffing ratios.

Table 9.4 Gross expenditure per child per week for foster and residential care, England

England				£ per child
	Foster care		Residential care	
	Cash terms	Real terms	Cash terms	Real terms
1991-92	120	140	790	924
1992-93	136	154	964	1,091
1993-94	152	168	1,067	1,176
1994-95	154	167	1,140	1,239
1995-96	163	172	1,231	1,300
1996-97	176	180	1,323	1,356
1997-98	191	191	1,378	1,378

Real terms: expenditure has been deflated using GDP price index, 1997-98 = 100
Note: GDP price index – see note at Table 9.1

9.18   Figure 9.2 illustrates how the costs in real terms of caring for children in residential care compare with foster care costs over recent years. The real costs of foster care have increased less steeply than residential care despite concern that the scarcity of foster carers might be driving up costs. These figures are consistent with the view that the supply of foster care might be increased by greater investment in fostering.

Figure 9.2 Gross weekly expenditure per child for foster and residential care (in real terms), England 1991-92 to 1997-98

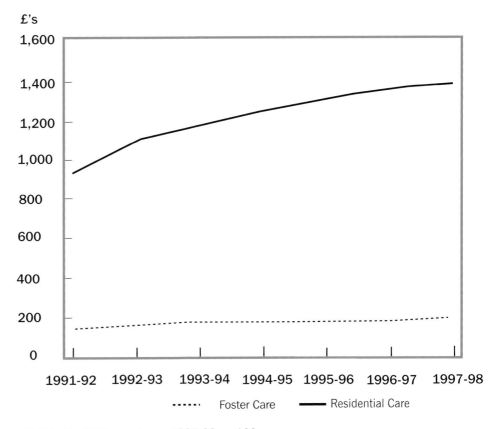

£'s

Deflated by GDP price index, 1997-98 = 100

The supply side – costs of foster care, residential care and secure accommodation

9.19   The average annual cost of children in need increases considerably if they are looked after by a local authority; the increase is several fold if they are looked after in residential care and greater still if the accommodation has to be secure. But costs vary greatly from authority to authority.

Costs of foster care, residential care and secure accommodation

9.20   Figures 9.3 and 9.4 show with respect to foster care and residential care the range of unit expenditure per child across authorities. Although in both cases most authorities cluster within or adjacent to the median range, a number of authorities are outliers and might, to their advantage, examine why this is the case.

Resource Planning

Figure 9.3 Gross weekly expenditure per child for foster care in 1997-98

number of local authorities

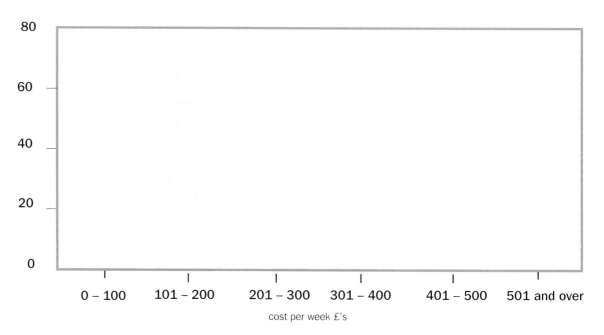

cost per week £'s

Figure 9.4 Gross weekly expenditure per child for children's homes in 1997-98

number of local authorities

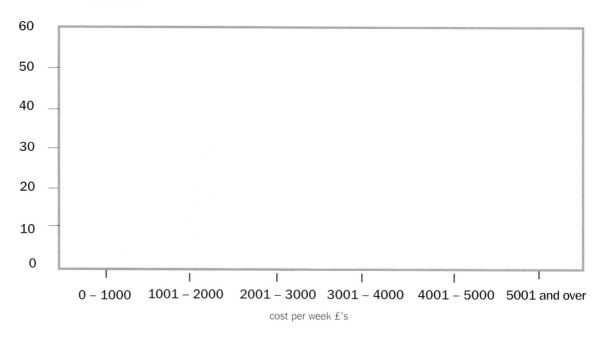

cost per week £'s

9.21   The unit costs are calculated using information on expenditure reported by
        local authorities to DETR and information on the placements of looked after
        children collected by the Department of Health. Part of the variation can be
        explained by differences in wage costs for which adjustments are made in the

Standard Spending Assessment (SSA) formula. Even so, the unit costs need to be treated with caution as not all authorities classify the expenditure data in the same way as activity data, and this may provide some explanation of the variation.

9.22   It is particularly difficult to get accurate figures on costs for foster care since there are so many different structures for schemes and payments. It is not clear whether local authorities include expenses and additional payments for children or only count the basic allowances. In conjunction with the forthcoming new collection of expenditure on children in need, we will be issuing guidance on the calculation of unit costs with a view to bringing consistency across authorities in how expenditure on children's services is allocated and apportioned.

9.23   There are large variations in the unit costs of providing residential care. This information, when combined with research findings *(Children's Homes: A Study in Diversity*, Sinclair and Gibbs, Wiley, 1998) suggest great variation in staff: child ratios, which do not bear a relationship to the type of home or, most significantly, to the quality of care experienced by the young people. Indeed there is some evidence that larger homes with high staff: child ratios might actually produce poorer care because large staff groups had difficulty maintaining consistency.

9.24   There has been a major programme of building to expand secure provision but at times this has meant significant upheavals to existing units with the capacity of the sector actually going down for a period. This has resulted in complex variations in expenditure in recent years which make comparisons difficult. The most recent information is for 1997-98 when the total gross expenditure on secure accommodation for children was £40.7 million. The cost of a place per child was £2,444 per week. Not surprisingly individual children requiring secure accommodation can make a significant dent in budgets. A clearer picture of expenditure trends in this sector will emerge in subsequent Children Act Reports as the building programme increases capacity significantly. As Figure 9.6 illustrates, there was a rapid expansion between 1996 and 1998.

9.25   Figure 9.5 uses data from the Safety of Children Survey conducted in July 1997 in response to the Chief Inspector letter to Directors CI(97)10. The survey sought numbers of approved foster care placements available to each authority and the numbers of children placed by the authority in foster care.

9.26   The ratio of numbers to places expressed as a percentage gives a measure of occupancy.

9.27   The occupancy rate for England had as a whole is 78%. The distribution between authorities is such that two thirds have an occupancy rate of 78% or higher. A number of authorities seem well supplied with foster placements but these do not offset the hard pressed authorities as much as the figures suggest because these are not in the right places for the children who need them.

Resource Planning

Figure 9.5 Occupancy rates of foster placements July 1997, by local authority

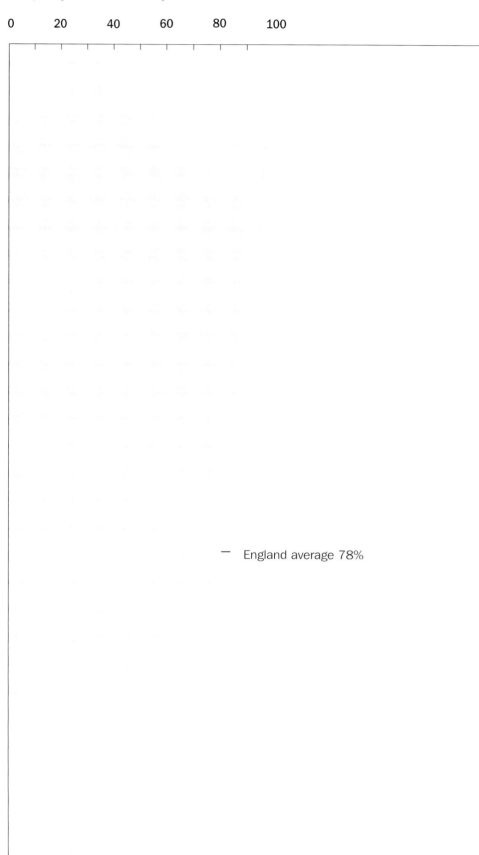

9.28 There must be some doubts about the accuracy of the figures, but individual authorities should re-examine their figures to ascertain the pressure on their foster care supply and see how, in broad terms, this ranks with all others. Creating available foster care places is part of the drive to increase placement choice within the Quality Protects programme.

Table 9.5 Number of places with approved foster carers at July 1997 and the number of children looked after in all types of placements at March 1997, by region

England

	Foster places available July 1997		Children looked after at 31 March 1997 in all types of placement		Ratio of children looked after at 31 March 1997 to the number of foster places available July 1997
	number	percentage	number	percentage	
All regions	**44,400**	*100*	**51,600**	*100*	**1.2**
North East	2,400	5	3,100	6	1.3
North West	6,100	14	6,500	13	1.1
Merseyside	1,400	3	2,100	4	1.5
Yorkshire & Humberside	4,700	11	6,300	12	1.3
East Midlands	3,900	9	3,400	7	0.9
West Midlands	5,200	12	5,600	11	1.1
South West	4,500	10	4,500	9	1.0
Eastern	4,000	9	4,500	9	1.1
South East	5,800	13	6,700	13	1.2
Inner London	3,200	7	4,600	9	1.4
Outer London	3,400	8	4,300	8	1.3

1 Excludes children looked after under agreed series of short term placements

9.29 Table 9.5 provides a basis for comparing the relative pressure for foster care places region by region. This can be done by calculating the ratio of looked after children at 31st March in each region to the number of foster care places available in the region. This ratio is given in the right hand column. It suggests that the supply of foster care placements in the East Midlands is relatively good and the greatest pressure on foster care placements is in Merseyside.

9.30 The ease of recruitment of foster carers depends on a variety of factors, including the reputation of the authority in supporting its carers and on the socio-economic characteristics of the community from whence they are drawn. The Department has shown that one key factor in the supply of foster carers is an inverse relationship to the number of women in full time employment. This relationship has been used to make an adjustment to the Standard Spending Assessment to take account of the extra costs to local authorities in areas where recruiting foster carers is more difficult. It would therefore be expected that the unit costs of foster care will vary between authorities. In addition some authorities, as a matter of policy, pay higher levels of allowances in recognition of the level of skill foster carers bring to the task. If this results in fewer disruptions and placement moves, it may be a good investment in terms of effectiveness.

Availability of residential care

9.31   Table 9.6 shows how the supply of children's homes places varies from region to region and how this relates to the numbers of children looked after aged 10 years and over, which is the age group most likely to create pressure for residential places. The ratio in the right hand column gives a measure of the relative pressure on places.

9.32   It would appear that the greatest pressure is in Inner London and the West Midlands and the least is in the South East.

Table 9.6 Places available in children's homes at 31 March 1997 and the number of children looked after in all types of placements at 31 March 1997, by region

England

	Places available at 31 March 1997		Children looked after at 31 March 1997 in all types of placement, aged 10 & over[1]		Ratio of children looked after, aged 10 & over, to the number of places available at 31 March 1997
	number	percentage	number	percentage	
All regions	10,900	100	30,800	100	2.8
North East	740	7	1,900	6	2.6
North West	1,600	15	3,900	13	2.4
Merseyside	560	5	1,300	4	2.3
Yorkshire & Humberside	1,300	12	3,700	12	2.8
East Midlands	760	7	2,100	7	2.8
West Midlands	870	8	3,600	12	4.1
South West	730	7	2,700	9	3.7
Eastern	800	7	2,900	9	3.6
South East	1,800	17	2,900	9	1.6
Inner London	600	6	2,900	9	4.8
Outer London	1,100	10	2,900	9	2.6

1 Excludes children looked after under agreed series of short term placements

Secure Accommodation

9.33   A major capital programme to increase the supply of local authority secure
        accommodation was completed in 1997. The main driver behind this has
        been the necessity to reduce to zero the number of boys aged 15 and 16
        who are being remanded into custody into prisons. This will allow for the
        implementation of Section 60 of the Criminal Justice Act 1991, which
        abolishes such remands.

9.34   Figure 9.6 shows the change in the supply of approved places. There has
        not been a straightforward increase from the previous baseline, partly
        because some secure places have had to be closed to allow for extensions
        and rebuilds on the same site to proceed. It has only been since 1997 that
        the numbers of places available has exceeded the 1988 level.

Figure 9.6 Places available and children accommodated in secure units at 31 March
1988 to 1998

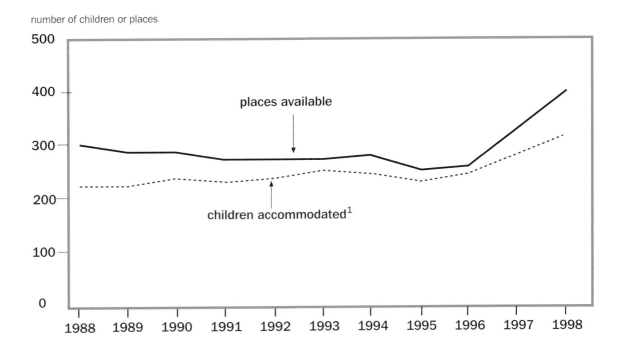

number of children or places

1 Includes children detained under S53 CYPA 1933

9.35   It can also be seen from Figure 9.6 that the numbers of children
        accommodated of necessity roughly follows the supply of places. It has been
        suggested that the use made by local authorities of secure accommodation is
        determined, not by need, but by supply. Table 9.7 and its associated Figure
        9.7 do not support this hypothesis, at least not on a regional basis. There
        are very marked discrepancies between the availability of secure places and
        the numbers of children placed in secure accommodation by authorities in
        several regions. Compare the relative under-usage by the North East and
        Merseyside with the relative over-usage by Yorkshire and Humberside and
        Outer London authorities.

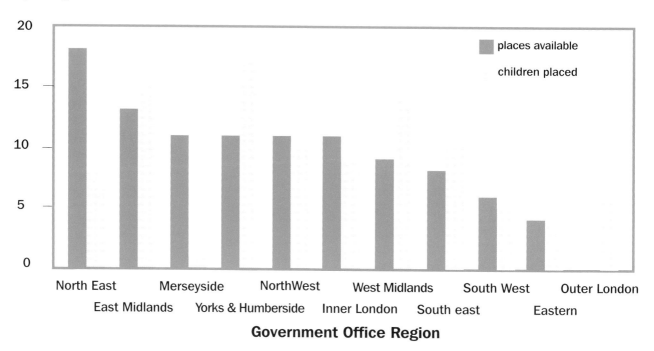

Figure 9.7 Percentage of places available in secure units and percentage of all children placed in any secure unit in the country by authorities in these regions at 31 March 1998

percentage of total at 31 March 1998

| | places available |
| | children placed |

Government Office Region

Table 9.7 Places available in Secure Units at 31 March and children placed in Secure Units at 31 March, by region, 1996 to 1998

England   numbers and percentages

| | places available at 31 March | | | | | | Children placed by region at 31 March, including those placed outside their own region | | | | | |
| | numbers | | | percentages | | | numbers | | | percentages | | |
	1996	1997	1998	1996	1997	1998	1996	1997	1998	1996	1997	1998
All regions	262	324	400	100	100	100	166	178	207	100	100	100
North East	48	48	72	18	15	18	16	15	17	10	8	8
East Midlands	12	32	50	5	10	13	22	17	31	13	10	15
Merseyside	43	43	45	16	13	11	5	5	3	3	3	1
Yorkshire & Humberside	37	37	45	14	11	11	18	23	35	11	13	17
North West	23	28	44	9	9	11	20	26	20	12	15	10
Inner London	24	24	40	9	7	10	7	17	19	4	10	9
West Midlands	16	36	36	6	11	9	15	19	29	9	11	14
South East	25	30	30	10	9	8	22	15	21	13	8	10
South West	28	38	22	11	12	6	20	21	10	12	12	5
Eastern	6	8	16	2	2	4	11	11	9	7	6	4
Outer London	-	-	-	-	-	-	10	9	13	6	5	6

Figure 9.8 York Index for children's social services

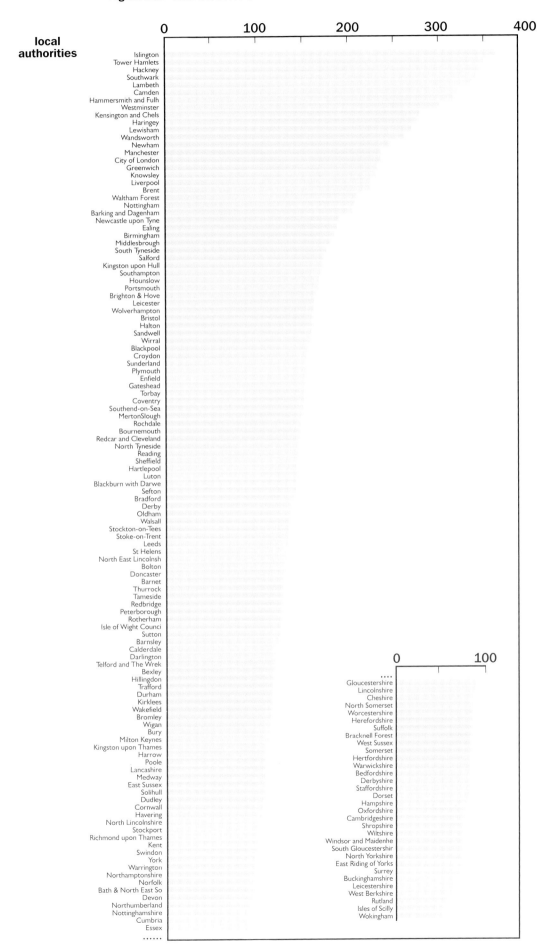

Underlying needs and demand

9.36   It is well established that the need for children's personal social services is
        directly related to social disadvantage. Social demographic indicators are
        used to construct a formula for determining how money from central
        government should be distributed between authorities to enable them to
        provide the standard level of children's services. This is adjusted for certain
        variations in supply side costs. This is called the Standard Spending
        Assessment (SSA) for children's services.

9.37   The formula for determining need for use in the SSAs, has been recently
        revised to take account of a 1996 survey by a consortium of MORI, York
        University and the National Children's Bureau to see how expenditure on all
        children in need is related to the social demographic characteristics of the
        areas where they live. The revised formula has led to a significant
        redistribution in the SSA for children's personal social services from 1 April
        1999.

        The socio-economic variables that make up the "York Index" are:

                Children in families on Income Support

                Children with limiting long-standing illness

                Children living in flats

                Population density

                Children in single parent families

9.38   Figure 9.8 portrays how this Index varies between authorities. The authority
        with the greatest index of need is at the top and the least at the bottom.
        There is a seven-fold variation between the greatest and the least need.

9.39   Figure 9.9 shows how we can use this Index of underlying need to begin to
        explain the variation in the rates of certain indicators of children's services.
        In this example it is applied to the rates at which children's names are placed
        on child protection registers. The line of bullets is the actual unstandardised
        rates per 10,000 children of children on child protection registers ranked
        from highest to lowest. The bars are the figures adjusted by the York Index.
        If the underlying need explained all of the variation the all authorities would
        be at the standardised average. Figure 9.9 shows that although there is
        something of a dampening effect, there remains very great variation between
        authorities.

9.40   Statistically it is estimated that the York Index of need can "explain" only
        20% of the variation between local authorities. The rest remains to be
        explained by variations in local practices and policies. Local policies and
        decision making appear to be the major determinant of registration rates.

Figure 9.9 Children on the child protection register per 10,000 population under 18 and standardised by the York index of need

Children on the Child Protection Register per 10,000 population under 18

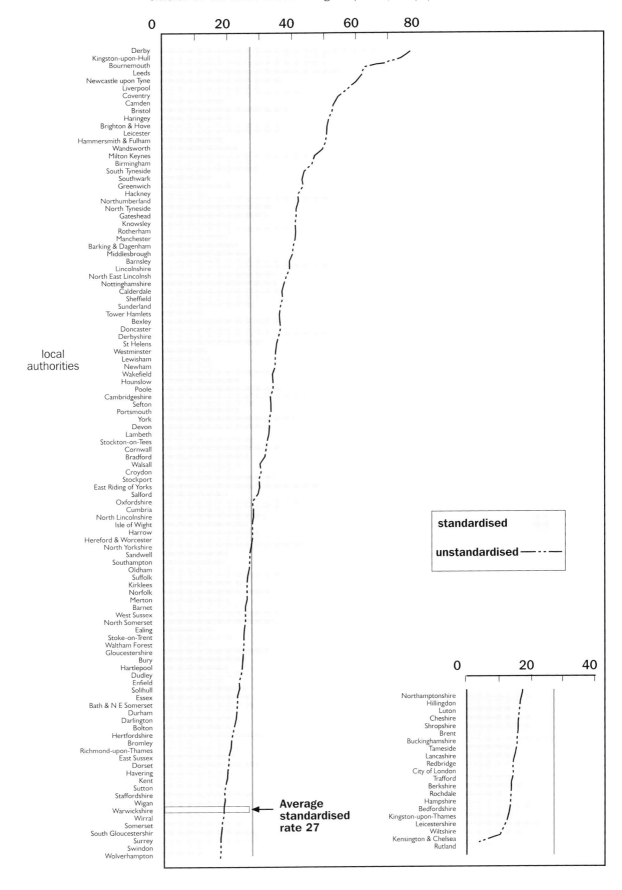

9.41   A similar analysis has been carried out on some other variables. This has shown that the York Index of need explains 50% of the variation between authorities on the rates per 10,000 of children placed in foster care. The Index is a relatively poor predictor of the rates for each authority of children becoming looked after but it accounts for much more of the variation between authorities of the numbers of looked after children at a particular point in time (31st March). This implies that local policies have a stronger influence over decisions to admit children to local authority care than the underlying need. Nonetheless, whatever admission processes operate, the numbers of children who end up being looked after for an extended period is more closely associated with underlying need. This suggests that there is scope to enhance the effectiveness of decision making at the point of considering admissions to care.

The use of resources for children's personal social services

9.42   Progress is being made on developing information about how resources for children's personal social services are used. The survey of children in need conducted by the consortium of MORI, York University and the National Children's Bureau in 1996 showed how expenditure was distributed between six categories of need. The six categories used were a proxy for need and were the best "common denominator" of categories that could be applied across all the 25 authorities in the survey.

9.43   The following two tables are taken from the report of this work entitled *A Model of the Determinants of Expenditure on Children's PSS* Centre for Health Economics, University of York.

Table 9.8 Numbers of children in the MORI survey in contact with social services, by age, sex and category of service, 1996

25 local authorities in England   number, percentages and rates per 10,000 population in age group

| | All children in sample | Rates per 10,000 population | Number of children | | | | | |
| | | | Looked after | | | Not looked after | | |
			Residential	Foster	Other	Child Protection	Disability	Other
All children in sample	74,493	302	1,984	5,892	1,805	4,406	8,330	52,076
Percentage	*100*		*3*	*8*	*2*	*6*	*11*	*70*
Boys								
All ages	41,230	326	1,253	3,062	943	2,239	4,991	28,742
0 – 4	9,426	281	28	591	221	81	670	7,102
5 – 9	10,602	335	101	766	237	718	1,555	7,225
10 – 14	10,398	352	525	977	196	547	1,456	6,697
15 – 19	10,804	339	599	728	289	160	1,310	7,718
Girls								
All ages	33,263	277	731	2,830	862	2,167	3,339	23,334
0 – 4	7,872	247	28	533	211	764	427	5,909
5 – 9	8,473	283	55	664	213	667	973	5,901
10 – 14	7,924	284	248	849	188	526	969	5,144
15 – 19	8,994	297	400	784	250	210	970	6,380

Table 9.9 Average annual cost in £ per child of children in MORI survey in contact with social services, by category of service, 1996							
25 local authorities in England							£s per child per year
	Average of all children	Looked after			Not looked after		
		Residential	Foster	Other	Child Protection	Disability	Other
All children	5,019	61,089	14,263	3,445	5,953	3,243	2,096

9.44   Table 9.8 shows how the numbers of children in need in the sample are broken down between these categories of "need", age and gender. From the information in this table it has been calculated that there are in the order of 350, 000 children in need in England at a given time.

9.45   It is noteworthy that 70% of children served by local authority social services departments come into the "not looked after - other" category. These are children who are being supported in their families for reasons other than their having a disability or whose names are on a child protection register. They represent the huge majority of children who do not come into high profile groups of children in the public care or for whom there is concern that they are at risk of abuse. It is interesting to compare the relative proportions in the numbers with the average expenditure per child of these groups as set out in Table 9.9.

9.46   Care is needed in interpreting these figures. They do not represent, for example, the average annual cost of a residential care place or foster home placement. They represent the average costs a local authority could expect to spend during the course of a year on each child whose need is characterised by one of the six descriptions. It would be fair to make a statement such as:

"For each child whose name is on the child protection register, a local authority can expect to spend, an average, £5953 (1996 prices) per annum."

9.47   These figures offer something of a bench mark for expected expenditure per child in each of these six categories.

9.48   Figure 9.9 shows that there is enormous variation between authorities in the rates of registration so the overall cost of child protection work for individual authorities can be expected to vary considerably.

9.49   Table 9.9 shows that, in expenditure terms, a child in need who is receiving social services, but who is neither on child protection nor disability registers, cost local authorities on average £2096 (1996 prices) per annum. Such children are in the huge majority of children in need but they make the least demand upon the public purse.

Departmental information on expenditure on children in need

9.50   The Department has been conscious that its information about activity and expenditure is skewed heavily towards looked after children and children on child protection registers - that is only about 20% of the children served by social service departments. It has, therefore, been looking at ways of achieving a broader picture.

9.51   The Department has successfully piloted with some 18 authorities a new statistical collection of activity and expenditure covering the full range of children in need. It works by taking a weeks census of all activity by social services on children in need. It is due to be introduced nationally in February 2000.

9.52   It will yield information about the numbers of children, volumes of service and expenditure disaggregated between nine categories of "need" (or "pressure to spend") and a number of service response categories. The collection will also include data on ethnicity and will be a vehicle for introducing better information about disability.

Planning

9.53   The requirement to plan services for children was written into the Children Act in 1996 by an amendment to permit the making of an Order. The Children Act 1989 (Amendment) (Children's Services Planning) Order 1996 and its associated guidance replaced the earlier guidance issued in 1992.

9.54   This chapter has presented information at a national level which is pertinent to the task of planning services for children. How expenditure is distributed between services and different demand, how it varies over time and between authorities are all issues which should inform planners. It is not the whole story - expenditure needs to be related to outcomes - but it is a significant part of planning.

9.55   The SSI study *Partners in Planning* (1998) reported that although the picture was mixed there was plenty of evidence of activity directed at collaboration between agencies. However the National Children's Bureau study *Children's Services Plans, Analysing need: reallocating resources* found that although there was certainly activity there was little to indicate significant changes in provision that could be directly related to the planning process. The study suggested that advances needed to be made in the more technical aspects of planning, in particular models for analysing need in ways which inform the allocation of resources, the better use of financial, information, and greater use of information and communication technology.

9.56   A recent SSI inspection of children's services planning arrangements confirmed the view that authorities are struggling to get to grips with planning children's services.

Messages from Inspection

Planning to Deliver: Inspection of Children's Services Planning (1998) found:

- the overwhelming impression is of a lack of strategic planning

- most Children's Services Plans were a statement of current activity rather than a driver in the planning process

- it was rare to find costings in Children's Services Plans and there was limited costing or sharing of financial information between agencies

- most LAs did not have a shared agency definition of children in need

- an audit approach was not adopted in reviewing existing resources and

- if services had objectives, plans did not identify performance measures. No current IT systems recorded outcome measures for individual service users

- performance and consultation was poor. There was some good practice linked to developments for children with disabilities where parents had been consulted

- it was rare to find evidence that comment/feedback had been collected and fed into the planning cycle

PART 3
Reports Mainly Derived from other Government Departments

Activity in the Courts

Introduction

10.1   Under the Children Act a range of court orders are available in what are usually termed "private" or "public" law proceedings. Private law proceedings involve individuals making arrangements for children. The Quality Protects programme does not cover private law proceedings. In public law, the local authority usually commences the proceedings, most commonly in respect of child protection issues.

10.2   The provisions of the Act allow some flexibility between private and public law court applications, including transfer from one to the other. But the principles of all applications are the same and are set out in Section 1 of the Act:

- the child's welfare shall be the court's paramount consideration

- any delay in determining the question is likely to prejudice the welfare of the child

- no order or orders should be made unless that would be better for the child than making no order at all.

10.3   Court proceedings under the Children Act are known as 'family proceedings'. That term also encompasses a range of proceedings under other legislation including:

- the inherent jurisdiction of the High Court in relation to children

- the Matrimonial Causes Act 1973

- the Adoption Act 1976

- the Human Fertilisation and Embryology Act 1990

- Part IV of the Family Law Act 1996

- Crime and Disorder Act 1998.

10.4   The main court orders available under the Children Act under the broad headings of private and public law are set out below. Orders concerning parental responsibility and financial matters are not included.

PRIVATE LAW	PUBLIC LAW
• Residence, contact, prohibited steps and specific issues (Section 8) • family assistance orders (Section 16)	• Contact orders (Section 8) • care and supervision orders (Section 31) • child assessment orders (Section 43) • emergency protection and extension of emergency protection orders (Section 44) • parental contact with children in care (Section 34) • secure accommodation orders (Section 25) • prohibited steps and residence orders (Section 8)

10.5   In any family proceedings in which a question arises with respect to the welfare of any child, the court may make a Section 8 order. This may come about either where a person makes an application as entitled or with leave of the court, or if the court itself considers that such an order is necessary. There are four types of Section 8 orders. These may determine with whom the child should have **contact** or **reside**, may **prohibit particular steps** being taken concerning the child without the consent of the court, or may order directions regarding **specific issues** concerning the child.

10.6   A family assistance order is available in exceptional cases and is the only order where the consent of the parties is required. The order offers short term support and advice to a family, perhaps following a divorce or separation, and usually where one or more Section 8 orders have also been made. The level of Family Assistance Orders made throughout the 1990s ranged from about 600 to around 1000 annually.

10.7   The numbers of orders made under the four options available in Section 8 in private law case are summarised in Table 10.1. This shows that from 1992 to 1996 Residence Orders made rose from just over 16,500 to over 27,600 but have reduced since. There was a similar rise in contact orders from just over 17,500 in 1992 to a peak of around 40,600 in 1997. In contrast, the number of orders made for prohibited steps and specific issues have not shown great variations during the 1990s.

Table 10.1 Number of Orders made annually – Private Law 1992-1998							
Private Law							
	1992	1993	1994	1995	1996	1997	1998
Residence	165151	22314	23919	25505	27660	25841	24204
Contact	17589	27780	31486	35280	40330	40660	39500
Prohibited steps	6103	6631	5971	5799	5783	5190	4307
Specific issues	1379	1563	1807	1741	2277	2108	1834
Family Assistance Orders	606	913	999	1039	1060	1009	864

10.8   Orders made in some of the public law options are summarised in Table
        10.2. This shows that generally through the 1990's, orders for emergency
        protection were around 2,500 per year with a peak of just over 3,000 for
        both 1994 and 1995, returning in 1998 to roughly the same level as 1992.
        Secure accommodation orders have shown annual variations from around
        950 to 1240.

10.9   Orders for care and supervision rose sharply after the implementation of the
        Act from around 3,300 in 1992 but thereafter increased more slowly from
        about 5,400 in 1994 to 5,700 in 1998. Care Orders more than doubled
        between 1992 and 1998, whilst Supervision Orders reached a peak in 1995
        but have fallen to below the 1992 level.

10.10   Relatively modest numbers of Prohibited Steps, Residence and Specific
        Issues Orders were made in public law proceedings. Residence Orders have
        diminished in numbers since a peak in 1994. These orders are most likely to
        arise as the option preferred to a care order in the course of care proceedings.
        Care orders have increased as public law residence orders have decreased.

Table 10.2 Number of Orders made annually – Public Law 1992-1998							
Public Law							
	1992	1993	1994	1995	1996	1997	1998
EPO&EPO EXT Orders	2423	2546	3144	3054	2565	2393	2473
PROHIBITED STEPS Orders	773	542	299	243	194	55	141
SECURE ACC Orders	964	1106	1240	985	1064	1086	1007
RESIDENCE_ Orders	1234	1470	1502	1081	1075	921	761
SPECIFIC ISSUE Orders	127	93	41	40	74	55	60
CARE Orders	2267	3221	4173	4240	4498	4537	4910
SUPERVISION Orders	937	1203	1325	1318	1161	1072	829

The guardian ad litem and reporting officer (GALRO) service

10.11   The guardian ad litem and reporting officer (GALRO) service was established in 1984. Each local authority was placed under a duty to administer a panel of guardians in its area with discretion to set up joint panels between authorities. Policy responsibility rests with the Department of Health.

10.12   The role of the guardian ad litem in public law proceedings is to safeguard and promote the welfare of the child before the court. The guardian is under a duty to report to the court on the child's wishes and on matters relevant to the proceedings. The guardian is under a similar duty in adoption cases to further the welfare of the child but the role of the reporting officer is adult rather than child focused. Here the function is to witness the parent's agreement to the proposed adoption and to ascertain that any such agreement is given freely, unconditionally and with full understanding.

10.13   With the implementation of the Children Act 1989, the powers and duties of the guardian ad litem in public law proceedings were more specifically detailed in accompanying Rules of Court. At the same time, the range of proceedings under the Children Act where it was expected that a guardian ad litem would normally be appointed was greatly extended.

10.14   The GALRO service is administered through panels of GALROs assisted by a panel committee which has mainly advisory functions. At present, there are 53 panels in England and 5 in Wales. Local authorities may contract out the day to day administration of the GALRO service to a voluntary organisation or other body. Currently, 3 panels in England and 2 in Wales are contracted out. These are all operated by different voluntary child care organisations.

10.15   National standards for the GALRO Service in England and Wales were published in 1995 and have been the subject of intensive follow-up both locally and under the lead of the Department of Health.

10.16   A national survey conducted in September 1998 showed that, in England and Wales, 1,091 guardians were panel members - comprising 839 individual guardians. Of this total:

- 641 (76%) worked for one panel

- 166 (20%) worked for two panels and

- 32 (4%) worked for 3 or more panels.

10.17   Of the 839 guardians:

- 656 (78%) were solely self-employed

- 142 (17%) were employed by local authorities and

- 39 (5%) employed by voluntary organisations

- 22 guardian panel members only undertook reporting officer work.

10.18   In total, panel management and administration was covered by 166 persons but many worked part-time and this figure represented 126 full time equivalent posts. There were:

- 59 persons designated as panel managers

- 5 persons assistant or deputy panel managers and

- 102 persons in administrative posts.

10.19   Guardians ad litem and reporting officers in England are appointed in around 13,300 proceedings annually. Of these, about 4,400 (33%) relate to adoption proceedings and the remainder are applications under the Children Act 1989. In Wales there are around 830 proceedings annually, with similar proportions to England relating to adoption and Children Act matters. Of adoption cases, around 61% involve a reporting officer and 39% require a guardian ad litem.

Policy developments

The Government review of court welfare services

10.20 In the Autumn of 1997, a review was conducted jointly by the Home Office, the Lord Chancellor's Department, the Department of Health and the Welsh Office of the provision of court welfare services currently provided by Family Court Welfare (FCW), the guardian ad litem and Reporting Officer (GALRO) Service and the Children's Division of the Official Solicitor's (OS) Department. It concluded that a new integrated service subsuming the work of each of the above services could provide:

- an improved service to the courts

- better safeguard the interests of children

- reduce wasteful overlaps and increase efficiency.

10.21 The Government decided that further detailed work involving practitioners and other users of the services should be undertaken to form the basis for public consultation. An announcement to this effect was made to Parliament on 16 February 1998 and set out the detailed terms of reference for the work as follows:

To identify the range of welfare services currently provided by the Probation Service, Guardian ad Litem and Reporting Officer Service and the children's work of the Official Solicitor's Department and other agencies in family proceedings, and to consider the scope for improvements to the effectiveness of their work through the creation of a new unified service.

To make proposals on the structure of a new service; to provide preliminary analysis of the estimated costs and benefits as a basis for public consultation; and to consider the implications for any new structure of the Government's plans to establish a Welsh Assembly.

10.22 At the end of July 1998, the Government announced the publication of a Consultation Paper "Support Services in Family Proceedings - Future Organisation of Court Welfare Services". Over 300 responses were submitted before close of consultation in mid November. There was strong support for the principle of a new unified service. On 27 July 1999 the Government announced that a new service would be set up as a Non - Departmental Public Body when the legislative timetable permits. The Lord Chancellor will have responsibility for the new service, the Children and Family Court Advisory Service. An inter-departmental project team is taking forward the preparatory work. The Queen's Speech confirmed legislation for the 1999/2000 Session.

The Children Act Advisory Committee

10.23 The Children Act Advisory Committee was set up in 1991 to monitor the operation of the Children Act 1989 and to comment on issues arising from its implementation. It published five annual reports which collected and disseminated information and statistics about Children Act cases and promulgated best practice. The Committee ceased its work in 1997.

Accompanying its final report in June 1997, the Committee published a Handbook of Best Practice in Children Act Cases. The President of the Family Division, The Right Honourable Sir Stephen Brown, described it in the Foreword as "an invaluable source of reference for the legal profession and others involved in this work".

Advisory Board on Family Law and Children Act Sub-Committee

10.24   The Advisory Board on Family Law was established by the Lord Chancellor in December 1996 and its members announced in March 1997. Its remit is:

- to advise the Lord Chancellor on issues arising from the implementation and operation of the Family Law Act 1996 and the application of the principles of Part 1

- to consider in particular issues arising from the Mediation and Information Meetings pilots

- to consider developments in research into supporting marriage and preventing marriage breakdown

- to maintain an overview of the working of the policy embodied in the Children Act within the family court system.

10.25   All appointments of members of the Board were for a five year period commencing 1 April 1997 and ending 31 March 2002. Arising from the Board's terms of reference, it was agreed that a Children Act Sub-Committee would be set up to give detailed attention to this subject. The Sub-Committee has assumed some of the responsibilities of the Children Act Advisory Committee which ceased operation in June 1997. However, it has a different remit and maintains a more strategic overview of the major policy issues and does not become involved in operational matters.

Care planning

10.26   Care planning is a crucial ingredient in the preparation of a local authority's application to court for a care order because it explains how the proposed order will be implemented. Before making a care order, courts have to be satisfied that the criteria set out in Section 31(2) are satisfied before turning their attention to whether under Section 1(5) making an order will be better for the child than making no order. This judgement will often rely to a considerable extent on the local authority's care plan. It is one of the most important documents considered by the court in care proceedings.

10.27   Following consultation, the Department of Health issued a local authority circular (LAC(99)29) on care plans and care proceedings under the Children Act 1989. It aimed to help achieve high standards of care planning within care applications at court and consistent practice regarding their preparation and use during and after the proceedings.

Early Years

Day care

11.1   Early Years services are intended to meet a variety of needs. Young children need opportunities to grow and develop socially, emotionally and intellectually. Parents and other carers may need help and support in helping children to develop. Good quality day-care provides opportunities for children in stimulating, caring, environments and also enables parents to take up work, training or education opportunities knowing their children are safe and well cared for. For some parents day care may be a lifeline, helping them to cope with problems and difficulties or providing respite that enables them to continue to be good parents. Early Years services are, therefore, an essential underpinning of policies for family support, as well as employment and welfare policies which aim to bring about social inclusion.

11.2   The Government launched its National Childcare Strategy in May 1998 with the aim of ensuring a range of childcare for children ages 0-14 years (up to 16 years for those with special needs) in every neighbourhood. The Strategy has the well-being of children at its heart, as well as offering equal opportunities to parents and helping them to balance work and family life. In addition, Sure Start, a new Government initiative to support families and children under four, will bring together a wide range of services including health care, childcare, early education and family support to improve life chances of children in disadvantaged areas. Through Sure Start, the Government will invest £452 million over the next three years in improving services for children under four and their families in 250 areas across England.

11.3   Part X of the Children Act and its associated guidance sets the standards for the registration and inspection of children's day care, which has usually been carried out by social services departments. There has been a steady growth of provision over recent years.

11.4   Figures 11.1 and 11.2 show that, over the last 5 years, there has been:

- a steady increase in the numbers of day nurseries; with an increase of 36% in the numbers of units and 45% in the numbers of placements

- a reduction of 8% in the number of playgroups and of 3% in places, possibly because of the increased availability of pre- school education in schools and nursery classes

- an increase of 13% in the numbers of registered childminders, but an increase of 21 % in places, possibly because childminders are registered to care for more school age children than in the past. (They may only care for 3 under 5s but can cater for 6 older children).

Figure 11.1 Numbers of day nurseries, childminders, playgroups, at 31 March 1987-1997, England

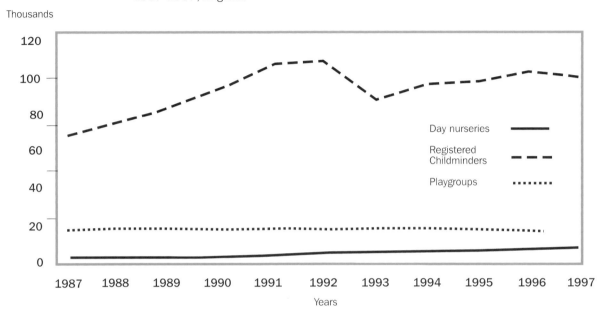

Figure 11.2 Day care places at 31 March 1987-1997, England

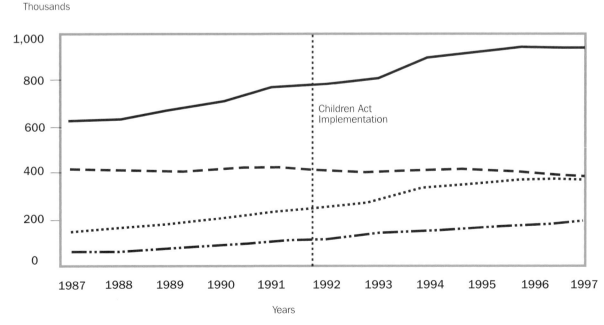

From 1992, figures for childminders are affected by the extension of registration to places for children aged 5-7

11.5   There has been an overall increase of 11% in the places available in day nurseries, childminders and playgroups.

11.6   No data is available on the take-up of places, although Early Years Development Plans are beginning to generate information about local supply and demand. Under the National Childcare Strategy, Early Years Development Partnerships have been extended to cover childcare and carried out the first ever audit of local childcare available, the needs of children and parents, and the gaps to be filled. Early Years Development and Childcare Partnership Plans for 1999-2000 set out their plans to create new childcare places.

Early education

11.7   In parallel with the growth of schemes and placements, there has also been a growth in the availability of early education. The Nursery Voucher Scheme was discontinued at the end of the summer term 1997. Since then, early education has been planned locally through Early Years Development Partnerships (now Early Years Development and Childcare Partnerships). The local education authority is required, in conjunction with the Partnership, to submit a Plan each year to the Secretary of State for Education and Employment for his approval. The Plan must set out how local early education and childcare will be delivered. It must set out the authority's proposals for meeting its statutory duty to secure a free good quality early education place, at least part-time, for all four year olds whose parents wish it. These free places have been available since September 1998.

11.8   The Government is also committed to doubling the number of free early education places to 66% of three year olds by 2002. £390 million has been set aside for three year olds from 1999 to 2002. The money available in 1999-2000 is restricted to the 57 local education authorities with greatest need. Funding will be available for all authorities from April 2000.

Out of school and holiday schemes

11.9   The Children Act introduced the registration of out of school clubs and holiday schemes for 5-7 year olds. There has been a steady growth in both numbers of schemes and in the places available and this is set to continue under the National Childcare Strategy through local Early Years Development and Childcare Partnership Plans.

Figure 11.3 Places for five to seven year olds; out of school clubs and holiday schemes, at 31 March 1992-1997, England

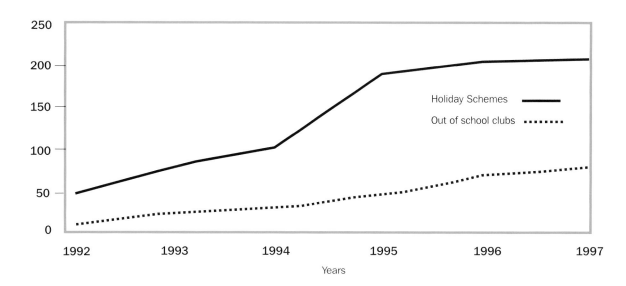

Transfer of responsibility to the Department for Education and Employment

11.10   During 1997/1998 it was agreed that the policy responsibility for provisions under Part X of the Children Act should transfer from the Department of Health to the Department for Education and Employment. This was accomplished on 1st April 1998. The responsibility for registration and inspection is currently a social services function. There is evidence of increasing collaboration at local level between social services departments, local education authorities, Ofsted, health interests and the wide range of private and voluntary organisations with an interest in young children. Following consultation the Government has announced its intention for the regulation of all children's day care to be brought together under a new arm of Ofsted.

Children in need

11.11   The Children Act places a duty on local authorities to provide such day care as is appropriate for children in need within their area who are aged 5 or under and not yet attending school. There is considerable variation in the amount and nature of day care, which is directly provided by local authorities or funded by them. Family centres are often use to support Children in Need and their families, but may not provide day care per se. At 31 March 1997 there were 480 family centres, an increase of 23% over the last 5 years.

11.12   An increasing majority of family centres provide services for children of all ages and their families but a significant minority (38%) provide services only for children under five. Family centres often provide a significant resource in work with families where there is a child protection issue, providing support and education for parents and also monitoring the safety of the children.

Annexes

Annex A: Social Services Inspectorate: Inspection Reports

1. Someone Else's Children: Inspections of Planning and Decision-making for Children Looked After and The Safety of Children Looked After (1998)

2. When Leaving Care is Leaving Home: Inspection of Leaving Care Services (1997)

3. For Children's Sake. Local Authority Adoption Services Part I (1996)

4. For Children's Sake. Local Authority Adoption Services Part II (1997)

5. Responding to Families in Need: Inspection of Assessment, Planning and Decision-making in Family Support Services (1997)

6. Getting Family Support Right: Inspection of the Delivery of Family Support Services (1999)

7. Removing Barriers for Disabled Children: Inspection of Services to Disabled Children and Their Families. (1998)

8. Planning to Deliver: Inspection of Children's Services Planning (1999)

9. Disabled Children: Directions for their future care (1998).

Annex B: References

1. Department of Health. Social Services Inspectorate (1998) *Partners in Planning.*

2. National Children's Bureau (1998) *Children's Services Plans Analysing Need: Reallocating Resources.*

3. House of Commons. (1998). *The Second Report of the Health Select Committee on Children Looked After by Local Authorities: Session 1997-98.* The Stationery Office. ISBN 0 -11-322101-0

4. *Childhood Matters*: Report of the National Commission of Inquiry into the Prevention of Child Abuse. (1996) The Stationery Office.

5. Department of Health and Welsh Office. (1997) *Sir William Utting. People like Us: The Report of the Review of the Safeguards for Children Living Away from Home*. The Stationery Office. ISBN 0-11-322101-0.

6. Department of Health (1998) *Modernising Health and Social Services: National Priorities Guidance 1999/00 to 2001/02.*

7. *The Government's Response to the Children's Safeguards Review. (1998)* Cm.4105. The Stationery Office. ISBN 0-10-14 1052-2

8. Department of Health. (1998) *Children Looked After by Local Authorities: Government Response to the Second Report of the Health Committee on Children Looked After by Local Authorities:* Session 1997-98. Cm.4175. The Stationery Office. ISBN 0-10-141752-7

9. Department of Health (1998) *Modernising Social Services*. The Stationery Office ISBN 0-10-14 1692 - X

10. Department of Health (1991) *Looking After Children: Assessing Outcomes in Child Care.* (HMSO)

11. Rodgers B. and Prior J. (1998). *Divorce and Separation: The Outcomes for Children.* (Joseph Rowntree Foundation)

12. *Supporting Adoption, Reframing the Approach BMF 1998*

13. Department of Health (1995) *Child Protection: Messages from Research (HMSO)*

14. Department of Health (1991) *Working Together Under the Children Act 1989.* (HMSO)

15. MORI/York/NCB *Survey of Children in Need. (1996)*

16. SSI/OFSTED (1995) ***The Education of Children who are Looked After.***

17. The Social Exclusion Unit (1998) ***Truancy and School Exclusion.*** Cm. 3957.

18. Gordon, Parker and Loughram. (1992) ***Children with Disabilities in Communal Establishments: A Further Analysis of the OPCS Investigations.*** (University of Bristol)

19. Gordon, Parker and Loughram. (1996) ***Children with Disabilities in Private Households: A Re-analysis of the OPCS Investigation.*** (University of Bristol)

20. Sinclair, Gibbs and Wiley. (1998) ***Children's Homes: A Study in Diversity.*** (Wiley)

21. Bebbington and Miles. ***The Background of Children who Enter Local Authority Care.*** (British Journal of Social Work vol.19, No.5 October 1989)

22. Department of Health (1999) ***A New Approach to Social Services Performance – Consultation Document.***

23. ***Support Services in Family Proceedings: Future Organisation of Court Welfare Services*** (1998) (Department of Health, Lord Chancellor's Department, Home Office, Welsh Office)

24. ***The Statutory Inspection Work of Local Authority Social Service Departments in Wales***: Monitoring Results for 1996-97.

25. ***Child Protection Register: Statistics for Wales***. (1995) (Welsh Office)

26. ***Home Office Supporting Families: A consultation document (1998)*** The Stationery Office.

27. ***Handbook of Best Practice in Children Act cases (1997)*** Lord Chancellor's Department

Annex C: Current or recently completed research on aspects of family support and support to parenting

1   Children in the Community with Behaviour Problems

Dr Stephen Scott
Institute of Psychiatry &
Professor Kathy Sylva
Institute of Education,
London

Starting date: September 1998
Length: 3 years

Enabling Parents

This research project offers support to parents who are finding the child's behaviour difficult to manage after beginning primary school. Many parents say they are keen to have practical advice on how to handle their children differently, and this study aims to provide that. The help to parents aimed to reduce children's behaviour problems on the one hand, and improve their ability to read and get on at school on the other.

Over a twelve week period groups of parents will watch videos of ways of handling problems, build up a repertoire of techniques and try these out at home. Parents will also be shown ways of helping their children to read and to correct mistakes in a specific and friendly manner. A community based sample of families who are experiencing stress because their children are being antisocial was selected, sixty offered the intensive intervention package while sixty acted as controls. There will be a further comparison group of children without these difficulties. Objective measures will be taken before and after the intervention and at a one year follow-up. If the programme proves helpful to parents, the methods will be disseminated to primary health care professionals and to teachers and special education need co-ordinators to enable the techniques to be practised widely. It is hoped that the programme will enable parents to set their children on a path to better adjustment and higher achievements.

Professor Jim Stevenson
Dr Edmund Sonuga-Barke
Dr Margaret Thomspon

University of Southampton

Strategies for Parents with Young Children with Behaviour Problems

The study aims to identify those aspects of parenting that improve difficult behaviour in young children and to find out what kinds of formal and informal supports have helped parents to cope. The families are part of the New Forest epidemiological study of child development and behaviour, a study of 1,047 children in the general population previously seen at age 3 and reassessed at age 8.

Starting date: January 1997
Length: 2 years

Children were allocated to one of four groups; those with no behaviour problems at either age; those who have problems at three but not at eight; those without problems at three who have developed them at age eight; and those with problems at both ages. That is: no problem, offset, onset and persistent problem groups. Fifty children from each of these groups were selected. Mothers and fathers were interviewed at home about how they have managed their child's behaviour over the past five years. The interviewers also asked parents about the support they had received from informal networks and from local services over their child's difficult behaviour; and how easy it had been to get help from services. This research draws on parents' own account and judgements of successful and unsuccessful techniques for handling their children's behaviour. This will provide important information for planning interventions to support families, based on parents' experiences.

2 Families with Disability

Sue Kirk & Caroline Glendinning

National Primary Care Research &
Development Centre,
University of Manchester

Starting date: January 1997
Length: 2 years

Supporting Families Caring for a Technology-Dependent Child

The study explores the experiences of families caring for a technology-dependent child and investigates how services from the health, social, education and voluntary sectors can be developed and co-ordinated to support this group of families. Advances in medical technology and policies of moving care from institutional settings into the community have led to increasing numbers of children dependent upon some form of medical technology (for example, mechanical ventilation) being cared for in the home. This involves parents in the provision of complex nursing care and highly technical procedures on a daily basis

A qualitative, exploratory approach was taken, with families being recruited via regional children's hospitals. In-depth interviews were conducted with 20 families caring for a child at home (and where feasible with the child her/himself) and with 40 service providers from a range of agencies identified by the families themselves. A small longitudinal sub-study of families with children awaiting discharge from hospital was also conducted. This study focuses on the process of commissioning and organising complex service packages to enable children to be discharged home. Interviews were conducted with families before and three months after discharge and also with individuals leading the discharge planning process and key service purchasers/commissioners in the areas to which the children are discharged.

Professor Gillian Parker,
& Dr Richard Olsen

Nuffield Community Care Studies
Unit,
University of Leicester

Starting date: May 1998
Length: 3 years

Parenting and Disability: The Role of Formal and Informal Supports

This study arises in part from the researchers' critique of the move to label the children of (some) disabled parents as 'young carers'. Instead, the intention is to understand more fully the types and amounts of both formal and informal support that is needed to support disabled people in their role as parents. The research involves two stages. The first stage involves interviews with 100 disabled parents and other family members. The focus is on the impact of impairment on: family life; the work responsibilities of family members; and the expectations placed on children. The families were traced using opportunistic sampling with a particular intention of comparing single versus dual parent households, and physical versus mental impairments. It is hoped also to explore issues of ethnicity; the degree to which the family is coping; recent and not so recent onset; and so on. Stage two involves 12 longitudinal case studies of families identified mainly through acute hospital wards. Here, the intention is to understand the 'journey' of a family from onset of impairment or illness onwards, with a particular focus on critical periods where support to enable continued parenting is particularly needed. The families will be visited on several occasions through the course of the research. It is hoped to include parents with traumatic injury, as well as those with mental health difficulties and chronic, disabling conditions such as multiple sclerosis or rheumatoid arthritis, in this stage of the research.

Dr Chris Hatton
Professor Eric Emerson
Sabih Azmi & Robina Shah

Hester Adrian Research Centre
University of Manchester

Starting date: January 1998
Length: 2 years

Stress, well-being, coping strategies and supports in Asian families with a child with severe disabilities

This study documents the levels of stress reported by Asian parents with a child with severe disabilities, examines the relationship between formal and informal supports and positive parenting outcomes in different Asian communities, and looks at the barriers to the effective provision of support to Asian parents. Asian children appear to have a higher prevalence of more severe disabilities than white children, but Asian people with disabilities are under-represented in residential services, partly because of the preference amongst users and carers to remain living as a family. High levels of stress among carers have been reported and these families would clearly benefit from support but there appear to be numerous barriers to the uptake of support services. These include material disadvantage, lack of awareness of services, language barriers, and a perceived lack of the appropriateness of the services to them. Two hundred Asian carers will be interviewed using standardised interviews about how they cope, the stresses upon them and the extent and meaning of the support they receive. A sub-sample of 30 carers will then be interviewed in greater depth to explore the psychological validity of the quantitative analysis to take further the meaning and relevance of the findings to the carers, and to explore constructive ways forward.

3   Children at Risk

Dr Elaine Farmer
University of Bristol

Starting date: October 1997
Length: 2 years 2 months

The fostering task with difficult adolescents

The study looks at foster carers' skills and the support, training and services they receive, as predictors of good outcomes in the care of difficult adolescents. Foster care is now one of the main services provided when serious difficulties arise with teenagers and their families and, over recent years, this has involved an increasing proportion of distressed and difficult young people. The disruption rate for these placements is high. At the same time the Children Act has emphasised the maintenance of links between children and their birth parents and the expectation that foster carers will work in partnership with them. At present, little is known about the key components of the fostering task with adolescents or what makes some carers particularly successful in looking after them. The research takes a consecutive sample of about 100 young people aged between 12 and 16 who face a new care episode as a result of concerns about their behaviour. The young people, their foster carers and social workers will be interviewed shortly after placement and again at twelve months, or at the point of disruption if this occurs earlier. The findings of the study provide evidence about the key requirements for training, support services and the selection of foster carers who look after difficult adolescents. They will be useful to those who have responsibility for planning and managing foster care services, to professionals who provide training and support services and to the foster carers who work in this very demanding area.

Professor Ian Sinclair &
Dr Ian Gibbs

University of York

Starting date: October 1996
Length: 2 years

Supporting foster placements

This study examines a large sample of foster placements, looks at the support received by foster families and children in relation to the support desired and to outcomes, after allowing for the characteristics of families and children. Although foster care has increased its share of 'looked after' children, concerns remain about the number of breakdowns, their effect on foster families and children, and the apparent difficulty in achieving change in the behaviour or educational performance of the children. Descriptions of support to foster families have been either small scale or too unspecific to assess its relationship to outcome. The project builds on earlier small scale work. About five hundred foster families were asked about the support they have received from services (eg training, social work visits, or work with the foster child). This was done using postal questionnaires at two points in time, thus allowing longitudinal statistical analyses of the factors associated with the outcome of placements. These findings were tested against an in-depth study of thirty families. The results of this study will be of value to local authorities in formulating policies to provide the types of support and training most likely to succeed in particular placements, and thus reduce the possibility of breakdown.

Alan Rushton
Institute of Psychiatry,
London

Starting date: December 1996
Length: 3 years 6 months

Parents who single-out and reject one of their children

The aim of this study is to advance knowledge on the psychological maltreatment of a specific group of children: those singled out from their siblings and rejected by their birth parents. The aim was to compare a sample of about 75 parents with a child identified by Health Visitors as singled out for rejection with a matched community sample of families without rejected children.

This study will have important implications for the identification of 'Children in Need' because of emotional abuse. First it will establish an incidence rate, which is an essential basis for planning services; secondly, it will provide more secure knowledge on the antecedents and consequences of this specific form of harmful parenting behaviour. This will help to refine the assessment of children suspected of being at risk of emotional abuse and help in the formulation of appropriate protection and care plans. Finally, more accurate and earlier identification of children singled out for rejection will allow the possibility of intervention before the child is exposed to long-term harm and when there is best hope of improvement in parenting. As little is known about effective intervention with these families, the study will provide documentation and recommendations on appropriate and viable strategies for ameliorative and protective intervention. Data gathering was mainly via home-based interviews with birth mothers, and also via screening questionnaires, standard measures of aspects of family life and interviews with child care professionals.

Professor Peter Wedge &
Dr Gwyneth Boswell
University of East Anglia

Starting date: October 1996
Length: 2 years

The parenting role of imprisoned fathers

This study identifies ways in which prison-based arrangements help prisoners fulfil their parental role, focusing on their experiences and their preferences for family support during their imprisonment. Fathers who are imprisoned are a particular sub-set of absent fathers, the majority of whom will return to home and family on discharge. The stress on families of imprisoned men has been well documented in descriptive studies; but the part that might be played by fatherhood 'education' or children's visiting schemes during imprisonment, has not been explored. The study examines prison-based initiatives for fatherhood 'education' and a range of provision made for father-child meetings. Interviews were conducted with about 180 prisoner-fathers. The sample was drawn from a geographical spread of establishments offering various types of parenting support schemes. Where possible the inmates' partners and their children were also interviewed. The views of service providers were also sought.

Christine McGuire &
Judith Corylon

National Children's Bureau,
London

Starting date: May 1995
Length: 3 years 3 months

Preparation and support for parenthood

Notwithstanding the fact that young people looked after by local authorities are often ill-prepared for parenthood, research has indicated that a high proportion of young women leaving care are pregnant or already mothers. This study is focused on pregnant teenagers and teenage parents who are being or have recently been looked-after, but aims to contribute to the general debate around adolescent parenting.

The study has 3 components: the *first* involved qualitative research in several local authorities in England. Interviews were held with policy-makers, young people looked-after who were pregnant or were parents and with their social workers or carers. The aim was to examine the services and support offered to these young people. In the *second*, quantitative and qualitative techniques are being used to explore the choices open to young people as they approach adulthood and how they are prepared for parenthood. Questionnaire information is being gathered from young people being looked-after and, as a control, from young people in mainstream schools. The quantitative research will be supplemented by in depth interviews and focus groups. The *third* component will involve the development of intervention strategies that might help prevent young women who are looked-after from having unwanted pregnancies and support those who do become parents.

4   Parenting in Poor Environments

Dr Deborah Ghate

Policy Studies
Institute of London

Starting date: May 1997
Length: 2 years

Parenting in poor environments

This study focuses on the issue of parental stress, taking as its starting point previous research findings which indicated that certain clusters of adverse socio-demographic characteristics are associated with parenting breakdown and child maltreatment. The study involves two phases: first a national survey, conducted by MORI, of 2,000 randomly selected parents living in areas of high material, social and structural disadvantage, together with a control sample of 500 parents living in 'average' environments. The second phases involved a qualitative study of about 45 parents from the survey sample who were bringing up children under different kinds of difficulty; for example, where parents have long-term serious health problems, are single parents, or are living in poor accommodation. The study will have as a central focus the identification of protective or buffering factors that help parents cope with these types of stresses. For example, parents' perceptions of the relative success of different strategies for coping with stress; their awareness and use of both formal and informal sources of support for families; their views on the types of support that would be most useful to them; and how such support might be delivered or reinforced. The central objective is to show how parents rearing children in stressful circumstances can be most effectively supported, and hence to contribute to current understanding of how best to implement primary prevention of parenting difficulties.

Professor Jane Tunstill
University of Keele

Starting date: September 1998
Length: 3 years

Family Centres: Their role and potential in co-ordinating formal and informal family support services

This project explores the extent to which family centres can act as gateways, and/or co-ordinating centres for services to Children in Need and their families, through an intensive study of twelve centres with different structures and approaches. Family Centres were specified in the Children Act as a service that local authorities should offer, and they were singled out by the Audit Commission as a potential solution to the current problem of restrictive, narrowly-focussed services. However, the term 'Family Centre' covers a wide range of seemingly disparate types of provision, including client focussed, neighbourhood focussed and community development projects, with little known about their relationship with formal and informal support networks, or their ability to facilitate access to either. In addition, while the idea that Family Centres might act as a gateway to services has attracted considerable support from both local authorities and voluntary organisations, they have remained under-resourced. The study maps the formal and informal support networks accessed at each stage by Family Centre participants and will measure any change over time. We hope to provide information that will be useful to everyone involved in and with family centres, including those who use them, the agencies who provide them, and policy makers and practitioners with responsibility for drawing up Children's Services Plans with their emphasis on integration and networking between services.

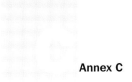
5 Normative Studies of Parenting in the Community

Marjorie Smith
Janet Boddy

Thomas Coram Research Unit
Institute of Education
London

Starting date: December 1997
Length: 2 years 6 months

A normative study of children's injuries

The frequency and nature of minor injuries, so called 'normal trauma', as well as the context and circumstances in which these injuries occur, is being studied in a community sample of children aged between birth and eight years. In particular the role of parental actions and expectations of child behaviour in causing or preventing injury is being investigated. The sample comprises a total population drawn from General Practitioner lists in a number of different locations including inner-city and non-metropolitan areas, and will be not less than 800 in number. Information on the nature of injuries and details of the context in which they occur is collected from families over a nine day period by means of incident diaries, daily telephone calls, or a combination of these methods. This is followed by a short interview with the caretaking parent, during which standardised measures of child behaviour, parents' expressed feelings and stress are completed. Parents in a smaller sub-sample of approximately a quarter of the families, selected to represent different child injury profiles and risks, are given a longer interview to explore parents' views on appropriate supervision, safety measures and expectations of child behaviour. As well as increasing understanding of non-accidental injury to children and policy relevance for accident prevention initiatives, the output from the study will be of value to those such as doctors, health visitors or teachers who have to make decisions about whether injuries observed on a child are within the normal range and consistent with an adequate level of parental care and supervision.

Marjorie Smith
Joanne Dixon &
Jeremy Robertson

Thomas Coram Research Unit
Institute of Education
London

Starting date: September 1996
Length: 3 years 3 months

Step children and step-parenting

The number of children who spend some time as part of a step-family is increasing. It is also clear that step-families are over-represented in some populations, for example, children looked-after, children subjected to abuse and young homeless people. Despite this there is little empirical information on step-families and step-children. Most of the research follows a 'deficit model', comparing step-families to other family types. This research aims to describe how children in step-families are parented, and to identify successful step-families – that is, to investigate variables related to the formation or functioning of the step family that are associated with a good outcome for the child. The study involves a representative community sample of approximately 200 step-families, each with at least one child between seven and eleven years of age, where the step-family has been in existence for between one and three years. The sample has been identified by means of a screening questionnaire, distributed to parents via schools, that focuses on changes children have experienced. The parent, step-parent and all children in the age range are individually interviewed at home. Existing data from a normative sample of families with children of the same age will be used in analysis for comparative purposes. The results of this study will be of relevance to all those professionally involved in working with step-families, or step children.

Recently completed research on workings of the Children Act

1 The courts and child protection

Pam Freeman
Joan Hunt

Centre for Socio-legal Studies
University of Bristol

Published November 1998

Parental Perspectives on Care Proceedings

A key principle underpinning the Children Act is the importance of working in partnership with parents. This includes families at the far end of the child protection spectrum where all preventive resources appear to have failed or a dramatic incident of abuse catapults them into the court process. This study examined the extent to which the new emphasis on working with families was reflected in the experiences of parents who are unwilling but key players in the legal process. It forms one strand of a project evaluating the impact of the Children Act on the use of the courts in child protection (study 12).

Joan Hunt
Alison Macleod
Pam Freeman
Caroline Thomas

Centre for Socio-legal Studies
University of Bristol

Published January 1999

The Last Resort: Child Protection, the Courts and the 1989 Children Act

The philosophy of the Children Act is that children are best cared for within their families of origin without recourse of the courts, and statutory intervention is a 'last resort' to be used only when other avenues have been tried and there seems to be no other way of ensuring a child's safety. This project concentrated on Part IV of the Children Act, the section dealing with care and supervision orders, and focused in particular on the use of compulsory intervention by local authorities in child protection cases, and the way in which these cases were managed by the courts. It was commissioned early in the Department of Health's programme of research on the Children Act and so was able to compare a sample of child protection court cases from before and after the Act, as well as looking at how key principle of the Act such as the 'no order' principle were being translated into practice in its first two years.

2 Services for children and families – The new concept of Children in Need

Jane Aldgate
Jane Tunstill

University of Leicester & London
Royal Holloway

Implementing services for Children in Need within the Children Act 1989

This study addressed a key aspect of the Children Act, the replacement of the relatively narrow concept of preventing children from being received into IOCA-I authority Care, with a broader duty under Section 17 to support families through the provision of services for Children in Need.

Jane Aldgate
Marie Bradley

University of Leicester

Publication Autumn 1999

Supporting Families through Short term Fostering

This study is about a particular kind of family support which local authorities can offer under section 20 of the Act. It provides for children to have short term breaks away from home, defined as no more than 4 weeks at a time of 120 days over a year with the same Carey Such short-term placements have traditionally been offered to families of disabled children, but this study investigated their use for other Children in Need.

Mano Candappa
Julie Bull
Claire Cameron
Peter Moss
Charlie Owen

Thomas Coram Research Unit
Institute of Education
University of London

Published 1996

Policy into Practice: Day care Services for Children under Eight

Whilst must of the Children Act concerns the service local authorities should offer to children who are in need, looked after or subject to court proceedings, the day care sections of the Act relate to services for young children (including childminders, playgroups and private day nurseries) have been registered by local authorities since 1948. The Children Act clarified the duties of local authorities with respect to such services and introduced some new requirements, including annual inspections (Part X), a three-yearly review of day care and educational services for children under eight (section 19), and a duty to make day care services available to Children in Need (section 17 & 18). This study investigated how local authorities had responded to the day care parts of the Act.

Matthew Colton
Charlotte Drury
Margaret Williams

University of Wales Swansea

Children in Need: Family Support under the Children Act 1989

This study examined the provision of services for Children in Need and their families under Part III of the Children Act, primarily in Wales but also in England. It was carried out before local government reorganisation in Wales in 1996, and looked at policies and plans in all 8 authorities followed by an in-depth study of services provided to Children in Need in two Welsh authorities.

Jean Packman
Christopher Hall

Dartington Social Research Unit

Published October 1998

From Care to Accommodation

Section 20 of the Children Act replaced the old notion of voluntary care with positive view of accommodation as a service that could be offered by local authorities to support families and Children in Need. Looking after children should be seen as a means of helping families, rather than as a last resort to be avoided wherever possible, and accommodation should be agreed on a voluntary basis in preference to using court orders to remove children from their homes. This study investigated how this new provision was being used, and how far the principles of working in partnership with parents and listening to children's wishes were being upheld.

Pat Petrie
Gill Poland
Sue Wayne

Thomas Coram Research Unit
Institute of Education
University of London

Play and Care out of School

Part X of the Children Act extended regulation of day care services to include those providing for school aged children up to the age of eight. Local authorities were also obliged to provide out of school services where appropriate to Children in Need. Little was known about this disparate group of services, which could include playschemes, after-school clubs, adventure playgrounds, out-of-school centres and day camps. This study was therefore commissioned early on in the research programme to describe and classify the different types of provision and provide baseline data against which the impact of the Act could later be judged.

Teresa Smith

Department of Applied Social Studies
and Social Research
University of Oxford

Published 1996

Family Centres and Bringing up Young Children

Family centres gained 'official' recognition in Part III of the Children Ac t1989 as part of the range of a family support services local authorities are required to provide 'as appropriate' in their area, and as a key element in preventive provision to meet need. This study explored how family centres operate and whether they are an effective way of providing services for families with young children, from the point of view of those who use them.

June Statham

Thomas Coram Research Unit
Institute of Education
University of London

Young Children in Wales: an evaluation of the Children Act 1998 for Day Care Services

This study was commissioned by the Welsh Office and linked to Study 6 in England. It explored the implementation in Wales of the parts of the Children Act relating to day care and the regulation of services for children aged under 8 (Parts III and X). It had a particular focus on the provision of services in rural areas, on respect for children's language and culture and on partnership with the independent sector, all of which are mentioned in Volume 2 of Children Act Guidance and Regulations.

Jane Tunstill
Jane Aldgate

London Royal Holloway and
University of Leicester

Publication forthcoming

From Policy into Practice: Services for Children in Need

This study was concerned with families who approach social services themselves for help, or who are referred by other agencies for services under Section 17 of the Children Act rather than because of child protection concerns or because they are disabled. It looked at the circumstances and needs of these families and the support they were offered, from the perspective of parents, children and social workers.

3   The protection of children at risk

Marian Brandon
Ann Lewis
June Thoburn
Ann Way

University of East Anglia

Published June 1999

Safeguarding Children with the Children Act 1989

The term 'significant harm' was introduced in Parts IV and V of the Children Act to mark the threshold at which courts could intervene in the lives of children. Before a court order can be considered, a child must be suffering or likely to suffer significant harm. This research set out to explore whether children were being protected from maltreatment and neglect under these new provisions, and to address concerns that the emphasis in the Act on working in partnership with parents might be placing some children at increased risk of harm.

June Thoburn
Jennifer Wilding
Jacqueline Watson

University of East Anglia

Publication forthcoming

Family Support in cases of Emotional Maltreatment and Neglect

This study investigated the relationship between children 'in need' and children 'in need of protection' because of concerns about neglect or emotional abuse. It builds on earlier research reported in 'Child protection: messages from research, which found that a large majority of children referred because of child protection concerns were quickly filtered out of the system and received no protective or support services. This was particularly marked for referrals for emotional maltreatment or neglect. The present study took a closer look at this type of referral, focussing on children aged under eight.

4   Children looked after by local authorities

Nina Biehal
Jasmine Clayden
Mike Stein
Jim Wade

University of York

Published 1995

Moving on: Young People and Leaving Care Schemes

Section 24 of the Children Act placed new duties upon local authorities to prepare young people for leaving care, and to advise and befriend young people to the age of 21 where they left care after their sixteenth birthday. It also provided discretionary power to offer financial assistance to young people in relation to housing, education, employment or training. Specialist leaving care schemes had been developed in some authorities since the mid 1980s, and this study set out to describe what such schemes offer, which type is most effective in helping young people using the schemes are better than for those who have not had access to them.

Roger Grimshaw
Ruth Sinclair

National Children's Bureau

Published 1997

Planning to Care: Regulation, Procedure and Practice under the Children Act 1989

Care planning is central to effective social work intervention with children and young people. In recognition of this, the Children Act introduced a new requirement that every young person who is looked after by the local authority should have an individual Care Plan, and that this should be reviewed regularly. The Guidance and Regulations accompanying this part of the Children Act constitute a set of national standards which spell out in unprecedented detail how local authorities should undertake this planning and review duty. This project collected evidence about the impact of this regulatory strategy on child care planning.

Peter Marsh
Mark Peel

University of Sheffield

Published March 1999

Leaving Care in Partnership

This research built on earlier work (eg Study 3) into how local authorities were meeting their duty under Section 24 to promote young people's welfare when they leave care. It focused on the important principle of partnership which underpins the Act, by investigating how young people leaving care could be supported by social workers working more closely in partnership with the young person's family and other significant individuals in their lives.

Recently completed research on children's residential care

Elaine Farmer, Sue Pollock

University of Bristol

Published 1998

Sexually Abused and Abusing Children in Substitute Care

This study considers how sexually abused children and young abusers are managed while living in residential and foster care. There has been little research in this area, and this study aimed to fill some of the gaps by examining the interventions provided for such children and the consequences of mixing these children with others.

Phase one of the study involved reviewing the case files of all the children who had been newly looked after during a specific period within two target local authorities. A comparison was made between the characteristics and care histories of the sexually abused/abusing children and the others. In phase two interviews were held with a sub sample of 40 abusing/abused children and their carers. The results showed that before entering substitute care the abused/abusing children were significantly more likely to have been placed on the "at risk" register than the other children, to have had previous care experience, to have experienced disruptive parenting, and to have had severe educational and social problems. The girls were more likely to have become pregnant. On entering care the background of sexual abuse or abusing was often overlooked or ignored, and a significant proportion of the children became involved sexually. However care givers and social workers tended to set high thresholds before taking action, particularly where sexual behaviour occurred outside the care setting. For abusers in particular there was little therapeutic help, although the study showed that the best outcomes in terms of behaviour were for those who had been given the opportunity to share openly about their experiences and feelings.

Elizabeth Brown
Roger Bullock
Caroline Hobson,
Michael Little

Dartington Social Research Unit

Published 1998

Making Residential Childcare Work

This research builds upon earlier research into the internal dynamics of residential care settings, and their impact upon staff and young people. The study aimed to discover whether a casual relationship could be found between the structure and culture of a children's home and effects upon outcomes for the home, and for children and families. The overall objective was to understand the characteristics of a 'good home' so that interventions designed to improve residential child care could be more effective. The study involved nine community homes in England and Wales, selected to represent the diverse range of residential homes for children.

Ian Gibbs
Ian Sinclair

University of York

Published 1998

Private Children's Homes

In recent years, the number of private homes for children have increased, while the number of places in local authority children's homes have declined. This study compares the clientele and other characteristics of eight private children's homes with a sample of children's homes managed by the local authority. Similarities and differences between the two groups of homes were investigated according to a range of factors, such as management issues, the distance between the home and the child's family, and level of contact sustained between children with family members. The study also compared the provision of education and therapeutic services, the role of staff in care planning and after-care, age profile of users, and levels of behavioural difficulty.

Michael Little
Siobhan Kelly

Dartington Social Research Unit

Published 1995

Life Without Problems? The achievements of a Therapeutic Community

This is an evaluation of the Caldecott Community, a residential community in Kent. General changes in the clientele and patterns of provision are identified since the community was established in 1911. For example, it appears that in the 1950s, the community catered for the needs of 'unhappy but clever' children. Over the next forty years, the focus shifted towards meeting the needs of children with severe behaviour difficulties and traumatic histories. The research undertakes a longitudinal analysis of groups of children admitted between 1986 and 1990, and compared with a matched group who underwent the selection process but were not admitted. The progress of all participants were followed up over a two year period.

Dorothy Whitaker
Lesley Archer
Leslie Hicks

University of York

Published 1998

Working in Children's Homes: Challenges and Complexities

This study analyses the perceptions and experiences of staff working in children's homes in relation to events and dynamics internal to the home, and in relation to the wider organisational and social network of contacts. The research was conducted in two parts: difficult events and their outcomes were explored with heads of homes. This was followed by an action research model in which staff were asked to set goals and explore factors which impeded or supported their achievement within the staff team. The characteristics of staff cultures which are likely to be receptive or, or rejecting of, good practice. Researchers also developed a profile of the knowledge, skills and personal qualities required to work effectively in children's homes.

Dione Hills
Camilla Child
Julie Hills
Vicky Blackburn

Tavistock Institute

Evaluating Residential Care Training: Towards qualified leadership

Following a number of high-profile scandals in children's homes in the 1980s, and growing concern at the lack of qualified staff working in this field, the Department of Health provided additional funding to improve training for senior staff in the residential care sector. This study evaluates the enhanced DipSW training programmes aimed at senior staff in residential care between 1992 and 1997. Course providers and local authorities received additional funding from the Department of Health to enable senior residential care staff to attend. The evaluation explores the extent to which the enhanced DipSW programmes met the needs of students, employers, and other agencies. The study also compared expressed satisfaction, course content and outcomes with other non-designated training programmes. Outcomes of the designated training programme were analysed at a local authority and service level.

Richard Whipp
Ian Kirkpatrick
Martin Kitchener
Dianne Owen

Cardiff University Business School

Published 1998

The External Management of Children's Homes by Local Authorities

Investigations into children's homes commonly highlight deficiencies in management practices. This study examines the difficulties and challenges associated with the management of heads of children's homes by senior managers in local authorities. Different models of management were identified from a sample of metropolitan, shire, London, and unitary social services departments, and their impact on the external management of children's homes analysed. The study also aimed to develop a framework for understanding and identifying 'best practice'.

Ian Sinclair
Ian Gibbs

University of York

Children's Homes: A Study in Diversity

This study aims to document variations in children's homes in their short and longer term outcomes, and to test whether these variations can be explained by factors such as child characteristics, staffing ratios, or the size of homes. The study contributes towards an assessment of the quality of care in children's home, and the impact of differences in quality on outcomes for staff and young people. The report analyses the relationships between the social environment of the home, the level of 'individual misery' expressed by young people, and the process of adjustment. Positive outcomes were associated with homes which were small and which had a low turnover. Clear roles and a shared agreement among staff about how the home should be run was also shown to be important. High staff ratios and high proportions of qualified staff were now shown to affect performance.

Amendments to the Children Act 1989 since 1 January 1994

Interpretation:

In this Annex references to "the Act" are references to the Children Act 1989. This Annex applies up to May 1999.

Amendment to Section 6 of the Act (Guardians: revocation and disclaimer):

Insertion of a new sub-section 3A by the Law Reform Succession Act 1995, section 4.

This amendment has the effect of revoking the appointment of a guardian on the dissolution or annulment of a marriage where the appointment is made by a parent with parental responsibility or by the guardian to take his place and the person appointed is his spouse unless a contrary intention appears in the appointment. This amendment operates in respect of a person dying on or after 1 January 1996 regardless of the date of the appointment or the date of annulment/dissolution.

Amendment to Section 8 of the Act (Residence, contact and other orders with respect to children):

Insertion of words "subject to sub-section 5" into sub-section 3 by the Family Law Act 1996, section 66(1), Schedule 8, paragraph 41(3).

Insertion of sub-section 5 by the Family Law Act 1996, section 66(1), Schedule 8, paragraph 41(4).

These provisions are to come into force on a date to be appointed in accordance with the Family Law Act 1996, section 67(3) and subject to savings in section 66(2) and Schedule 9 of the Family Law Act 1996. When in force, these new words and sub-section will provide that powers under the Children Act which are exercisable in family proceedings shall also be exercisable in relation to a child without any such proceedings having been commenced or any application made to the court, where there has been a statement of marital breakdown lodged at Court under section 5 of the Family Law Act 1996 with respect to a marriage which the child is a child of the family and it may become possible for an application for divorce or separation to be made by reference to that statement.

Paragraph (c) and (f) of sub-section 4 repealed by Family Law Act 1996, section 66 (1), (3), Schedule 8, paragraph 60(1), Schedule 10 (subject to savings in section 66(2) and Schedule 9 of the Family Law Act 1996).

This removes references to the Domestic Violence and Matrimonial Proceedings Act 1976 and the Matrimonial Homes Act 1983 which have both been repealed.

New paragraph (h) inserted into sub-section 4 by the Family Law Act 1996, section 66(1), Schedule 8, paragraph 60(1).

This provides that family proceedings for the purpose of the Act includes proceedings under the Family Law Act 1996.

New paragraph (i) inserted into sub-section 4 by the Crime and Disorder Act 1998, section 119, Schedule 8, paragraph 68.

This provides that family proceedings for the purpose of the Act includes proceedings under section 11 and section 12 of the Crime and Disorder Act 1998. In force from 30 September 1998

Amendment to Section 24 of the Act (Advice and assistance for certain children):

Insertion of the words "Health Authority and Special Heath Authority" into sub-section (2)(d)(i) and (12)(b) by the Health Authorities Act 1995, section 2(1), Schedule 1, p. 118(4).

These amendments provide that a person qualifying for advice and assistance can now include a person accommodated by either a health authority or a special health authority.

New Section 38A to the Act (Power to include exclusion requirement in interim care order):

New Section 38B to the Act (Undertakings relating to interim care orders):

Both Sections inserted prospectively from a date to be appointed by the Family Law Act 1996, section 52, Schedule 6, paragraph 1.

These amendments implement the recommendations of the Law Commission's report on Domestic Violence and Occupation of the Family Home. They allow the Court to make short term emergency ouster orders. These sections also provide that where the Court has power to include an exclusion requirement in an interim care order the Court may instead accept undertaking. Whilst a power of arrest may attach to an exclusion requirement it cannot attach to an undertaking. Both are enforceable as if there were orders of the Court.

Amendment to Section 39 of the Act (Discharge and variation etc of care orders and supervision orders):

Insertion of new sub-section 3A and 3B from 1 October 1997 by Family Law Act 1996, section 52, Schedule 6, paragraph 2.

These amendments make provision for applications as to the discharge and variation of an interim care order so far as it imposes an exclusion requirement or confers the power to arrest.

Insertion of a new Section 44A to the Act (Power to include exclusion requirement in emergency protection order):

Inserted from 1 October 1997 by Family Law Act 1996, section 52, Schedule 6, paragraph 3.

This amendment gives power to include exclusion requirements in emergency protection orders.

Insertion of a new Section 44B to the Act (Undertakings relating to emergency protection orders):

Inserted from 1 October 1997 by Family Law Act 1996, section 52, Schedule 6, paragraph 3.

This amendment gives power to include undertakings relating to emergency protection orders.

Amendment to Section 45 of the Act (Duration of emergency protection orders and other supplementary provisions):

Insertion of a new subparagraph 8(A) and 8(B) from 1 October 1997 by Family Law Act 1996, section 52, Schedule 6, paragraph 4.

This amendment adds the power to vary or discharge an order insofar as it imposes an exclusion requirement and/or a power of arrest that may have been attached to an exclusion order.

Amendment to Section 47 of the Act (Local authority's duty to investigate):

Insertion of a new subsection 1(a)(iii) and words in subsection 3(a) by Crime and Disorder Act 1998 section 15(4), 119, Schedule 8, paragraph 69.

In force from 30 September 1998. This amendment will impose a duty to investigate on the local authority when informed that a child who lives in, or is found in, their area has contravened a ban imposed by curfew notice within the meaning of Chapter 1, Part 1 of the Crime and Disorder Act 1998.

Insertion of words "In the case" to "the information" into section 47(1) of the Act, by Section 15(4)(b) of the Crime and Disorder Act 1998.

In force from 30 September 1998. This will provide that where a local authority is making enquiries with regards to investigating a child who has contravened a ban imposed by curfew notice, those enquiries are commenced as soon as practicable and in any event within 48 hours of the authority receiving the information.

Insertion of words "or section 11" and "(child safety orders)" into subsection (3) of section 47, by the Crime and Disorder Act 1998 section 119, Schedule 8, paragraph 69.

In force from 30 September 1998. This amendment provides that any enquiries made by the local authority directed towards establishing whether the authority should make any application to the Court or exercise any of their powers, now will include new powers under section 11 of the Crime Disorder Act 1998 being child safety orders.

Amendment to Section 53 of Act (Provision of community homes by local authorities):

Insertion of subsections 3A and 3B (and consequential amendments into sub-section 3) by sections 22(2)(a),(b) of the Public Order Act 1994.

This amendment provides that a local authority may make arrangements for the management by another person of accommodation provided by the local authority for the purpose of restricting the liberty of the child. Also provides that where a local authority is to be responsible for the management of a community home provided by a voluntary organisation, the local authority may, with the consent of the body of managers (under the instrument of management) make arrangements for the management of the home by another person where the accommodation is for the purpose of restricting the liberty of a child.

Amendment of Section 63 of the Act (Children not to be cared for and accommodated in unregistered children's homes):

Substitution of a new subsection 6 by the Education Act 1996, section 582(1), Schedule 37, paragraph 86.

Provides that an independent school is a children's home at any time if, at that time, accommodation is provided for 3 or more children at the school for greater than 295 days over a period of 2 years, or that it is intended to provide accommodation for more than 3 children at the school for more than 295 days, unless the school is registered as a school under section 347(1) of the Education Act 1996.

Insertion of a new Section 87A into Act (Suspension of duty under section 87(3)):

Insertion of a new Section 87B into Act (Duties of inspectors under section 87A):

Both Sections inserted by the Deregulation and Contracting out Act 1994, Section 38.
Both sections drafted after discussion with the independent schools joint council.

These new sections enable an independent school to opt for inspection for welfare purposes by a person other than the local authority. The reasoning behind these sections is that it is right that there should be inspection but that this should be undertaken by bodies which have the approval of the Secretary of State and not just be the social services. Section 87B provides that the Secretary of State may impose such requirements relating to the person appointed as he wishes and other provisions in relation to the appointees duties.

Amendment to Schedule 2 of the Act (Local authority support for children and families):

Insertion of a new paragraph 1A by Children Act 1989 (Amendment) Children's Services Planning) Order 1996 SI 1996/785, art. 2.

This amends Schedule 2 of the Children Act 1989 so that after paragraph 1 there is inserted paragraph 1A "Children's services plans". This requires local authorities to prepare and publish plans for the provision of children's services in their area and keep those plans under review. In preparing or updating their plans local authorities are required to consult health and education authorities, certain voluntary organisations, police, probation services and other relevant bodies. The Secretary of State may require the local authority to submit these plans to him at any time.

Amendment to Schedule 4 of the Act (Management and conduct of community homes):

Insertion of new words into paragraph 4 and 5 of Part II, of Schedule 4 by Criminal Justice and Public Order Act 1994,s. 22(1), (3).

These are consequential amendments as a result of insertion of 53(3B). These provide that where an assisted community home is managed by someone else the functions of a home's responsible body shall be exercised through the managers except in so far as under section 53(3B) any of the accommodation is managed by another person. These also provide that liability incurred or property acquired by a home's managers is incurred or acquired by the responsible body and this also applies where under 53(3B) the home is being managed by another person.

Amendment to Schedule 5, Part II of the Act (Regulations as to Voluntary Homes):

Repeal of par. 7(2)(f) and insertion of par. 7(2)(ff) by Criminal Justice and Public Order Act 1994,ss 19(2)(a), 168(3), Schedule 11.

This provides that the Secretary of State may make regulations and that these regulations may, in particular, require the approval of the Secretary of State for the provision and use of accommodation for the purpose of restricting liberty of children in homes and impose other requirements as to the placing of a child in such accommodation.

Amendment to Schedule 6 (Registered Children's Homes), Part II of the Act (Regulations):

Repeal of par. 10(2)(j) and insertion of par. 10(2)(jj) by Criminal Justice and Public Order Act 1994,ss 19(2)(b), 168(3), Schedule 11.

This provides that the Secretary of State may make regulations and that these regulations may, in particular, require the approval of the Secretary of State for the provision and use of accommodation for the purpose of restricting liberty of children in homes and impose other requirements as to the placing of a child in such accommodation.

Amendments to Regulations made under the Children Act 1989 since 1 January 1994

Interpretation:

In this Annex references to the "principal regulations" are to those Regulations that are being amended by subsequent Regulations and are in bold at the start of each section.

Amendment to the Adoption Agencies Regulations 1983:

Amending Regulation: Regulation 2(1) of the Children (Protection from Offenders) (Miscellaneous Amendments) Regulations 1997

This amends regulation 1 (interpretation) of the principal regulations to include a definition of "specified offence" – this means an offence specified in Schedule 2.

Amending Regulation: Regulation 2(9) of the Children (Protection from Offenders) (Miscellaneous Amendments) Regulations 1997.

This inserts Schedule 2 into the principal regulations. Schedule 2 lists offences that are "specified offences" in England, Scotland, Wales and Northern Ireland.

Amending Regulation: Regulation 2(3)(a-c) of the Children (Protection from Offenders) (Miscellaneous Amendments) Regulations 1997

This makes certain minor changes to Regulation 8 (Adoption agency's duties in respect of a prospective adopter) in the principal regulations which include making certain actions subject to regulation 8A.

Amending Regulation: Regulation 2(4) of the Children (Protection from Offenders) (Miscellaneous Amendments) Regulations 1997

This inserts a new section 8A into the principal regulations, which is entitled "criminal convictions of a prospective adopter".

Effect:

The effect of the above amendments taken together is that an adoption agency is required to obtain information about any criminal convictions and cautions when considering whether a person may be suitable to be an adoptive parent. It also provides that a person is not to be regarded as suitable to be an adoptive parent if he has been convicted of, or given a caution in respect of, certain serious offences contained in Schedule 2 and known as special offences. Also the local authority must carry out a police check when investigating an application for an adoption order in non-agency cases.

Amending Regulation: Regulation 2(2) of the Adoption Agencies and Children (Arrangements for Placements and Reviews) (Miscellaneous Amendments) Regulations 1997

This substitutes into regulation 1(3) (interpretation) of the principal regulations, a new definition of the Act as "the Adoption Act 1976 and for "the 1975 Act" there is inserted "the Children Act 1989".

Amending Regulation: Regulation 2(4) of the Adoption Agencies and Children (Arrangements for Placements and Reviews) (Miscellaneous Amendments) Regulations 1997

This inserts into the principal regulations a new regulation 5 entitled "Establishment of adoption panel and appointment of members"; a new regulation 5A entitled "Tenure of office holders"; and a new regulation 5B "Establishment of new panel on 1 November 1997". These amendments make provision for membership of adoption panels and for the tenure of office members. In particular they provide for the:

appointment of a vice-chairman (as well as the chairman) of the panel
for the panel to include at least three independent persons including where practicable, an adoptive parent or adopted person
for a written record of the panel's reasons for its recommendations and;
for the establishment of a joint panel by no more than 3 local authorities where appropriate.

The amendments also provide for a maximum 3 year term of office for members and for their eligibility for one consecutive re-appointment; for the cessation of membership of panel established before 1st November 1997 and for the establishment of new panels from that date.

Amending Regulation: Regulation 2(6) of the Adoption Agencies and Children (Arrangements for Placements and Reviews) (Miscellaneous Amendments) Regulations 1997

This substitutes new paragraphs (g), (h) and (i) for sub-paragraph (g) in regulation 8(2) (adoptive agency's duties – prospective adopters) of the principal regulations. These amendments provide that the adoptive agency must:

prepare a written assessment report of prospective adopters suitability to be an adoptive parent
notify the adopter that his application is being referred to the panel
send a copy of the assessment inviting observations within 28 days and
at the end of this period pass all information to the adoption panel.

Amending Regulation: Regulation 2(10) of the Adoption Agencies and Children (Arrangements for Placements and Reviews) (Miscellaneous Amendments) Regulations 1997

This inserts a new regulation 11A into the principal regulations entitled "Adoption agency decisions and notifications – prospective adopters". This provides that no member of an adoption panel shall take part in any decision made by the Agency under regulation 10(1)(b) of the principal regulations. It also provides that notification of adoption proceedings should be in writing and any decision that someone is not suitable should be notified to the prospective adopter giving him an opportunity to make representations before a final decision is taken.

Amending Regulation: Regulation 2(11) of the Adoption Agencies and Children

(Arrangements for Placements and Reviews) (Miscellaneous Amendments) Regulations 1997

This inserts the following amendments into regulation 12 of the principal regulations:

New sub-paragraphs (aa) and (aaa) after sub-paragraph (a) into sub-paragraph (2). This provides a requirement to notify the parent or guardian of the child (if their whereabouts are known to the agency) in writing of the proposed placement for adoption unless the parent or guardian has made a declaration of no further involvement. It also requires the father to be notified if he does not have parental responsibility for the child when the agency feels that this is in the child's best interests and the father's whereabouts are known;
New sub-paragraph (2)(j). This provides for appointments to be made for the regular examination and assessment by a registered medical practitioner of the child's health;
New sub-paragraph (2)(k). This provides for a review of the placement for adoption of the child;
New paragraphs (3) & (4). This makes further provisions for the conduct of the review and notification of results of the review.

Amending Regulation: Regulation 2(13) of the Adoption Agencies and Children (Arrangements for Placements and Reviews) (Miscellaneous Amendments) Regulations 1997

This inserts a new regulation 13A into the principal regulations entitled "Information on Adoption". This makes provision for information about the child to be given by the agency to the adopters once the adoption order has been made and for the adopters to be advised that the information should be made available to the child no later than his 18th birthday.

Amending Regulation: Regulation 2(14) of the Adoption Agencies and Children (Arrangements for Placements and Reviews) (Miscellaneous Amendments) Regulations 1997

This adds an additional paragraph (4) at the end of regulation 14 (confidentiality and preservation of case records) of the principal regulations. This makes provision for preserving adoption records, etc., and minimising the risk of damage from fire or water.

Amending Regulation: Regulation 2(15) of the Adoption Agencies and Children (Arrangements for Placements and Reviews) (Miscellaneous Amendments) Regulations 1997

This makes changes to regulation 15(1) (access to case records and disclosure of information) into the principal regulations. This makes provision for the disclosure of confidential records to persons appointed by the adoption agency to consider complaints.

Amending Regulation: Regulation 2(16) of the Adoption Agencies and Children (Arrangements for Placements and Reviews) (Miscellaneous Amendments) Regulations 1997

This substitutes a new regulation 17 into the principal regulations. This makes provision for the exchange of information between agencies where responsibility is being transferred.
Amending Regulation: Regulation 2(17) of the Adoption Agencies and Children (Arrangements for Placements and Reviews) (Miscellaneous Amendments) Regulations 1997

This adds a new paragraph 12 and 12A of Part 1 of the Schedule to the principal regulations. This provides for any special health or education needs of the child to be identified and for consideration to be given to how those needs are to be met.

Amending Regulation: Regulation 2(18) of the Adoption Agencies and Children (Arrangements for Placements and Reviews) (Miscellaneous Amendments) Regulations 1997

This adds a new sub-paragraph (dd) after paragraph 3(d) of Part II of the Schedule (matters to be covered in report on the childs health) of the principal regulations. This also provides for any special health or education needs of the child to be identified and for consideration to be given to how those needs are to be met.

Amending Regulation: Regulation 2(20) of the Adoption Agencies and Children (Arrangements for Placements and Reviews) (Miscellaneous Amendments) Regulations 1997

This adds a new Part VIII to the Schedule in the principal regulations entitled "considerations to be included in review". This deals with what matters should be taken into account on review.

Amendment to the Foster Placement (Children) Regulations 1991

Amending Regulation: Regulation 3(2) of the Children (Protection from Offenders) (Miscellaneous Amendments) Regulations 1997

This amends regulation 1 (interpretation) of the principal regulations to include a definition of "specified offence" – this means an offence specified in Schedule 2.

Amending Regulation: Regulation 3(3)(a) of the Children (Protection from Offenders) (Miscellaneous Amendments) Regulations 1997

This amends regulation 3 (approval of foster parents) of the principal regulations and makes approval now subject to paragraphs (3), (4) and (4A).

Amending Regulation: Regulation 3(3)(b) of the Children (Protection from Offenders) (Miscellaneous Amendments) Regulations 1997

Inserts a new regulation 4A into the principal Regulations. 4A provides that a person shall not be regarded as suitable to act as a foster parent if he, or any member of his household over the age of 18, has been convicted of a specified offence or has been cautioned in respect of any such offence which at the time the caution was given he admitted.

Amending Regulation: Regulation 3(4) of the Children (Protection from Offenders) (Miscellaneous Amendments) Regulations 1997

This substitutes a new paragraph 9 into Schedule 1 of the principal regulations entitled "any previous criminal convictions and any cautions given by a constable in respect of criminal offences relating either to him or any other member of his household over the age of 18".

Amending Regulation: Regulation 3(5) of the Children (Protection from Offenders) (Miscellaneous Amendments) Regulations 1997

This inserts Schedule 4 into the principal regulations which defines what a specified offence is.

Amending Regulation: Regulation 2 of the Children (short-term placements) (Miscellaneous Amendments) Regulations 1995

This substitutes a new regulation 9 into the principal regulations which modifies the total length of time for which a series of short term placements may last and still be regarded as one placement and also modifies the requirements for visits to supervise a series of short term placements.

Amendment to the Children's Homes Regulations 1991

Amending Regulation: Regulation 4(2) of the Children (Protection from Offenders) (Miscellaneous Amendments) Regulations 1997

This inserts a new sub-paragraph (3) into regulation 5 (staffing of children's homes) of the principal regulations. This ensures that the responsible authority shall, where practicable, obtain information about previous criminal convictions/cautions before employing or engaging the services of a person in a children's home in a position which involves substantial and unsupervised access to children on a sustained or regular basis.

Amending Regulation: Regulation 2 of the Children (Homes and Secure Accommodation) (Miscellaneous Amendments) Regulations 1996

This amends regulation 2 of the principal regulations by including a reference in the definition of "maintained community home" to include a reference to such homes managed by the local authority by persons authorised by local authorities or, in relation to secure accommodation, by other persons with whom local authorities have made arrangements to manage that accommodation.

Amending Regulation: Regulation 2 of the Children Homes Amendment Regulations 1994

This amends regulation 14 (fire precautions) of the principal regulations. It substitutes a new sub-paragraph (2) which requires the responsible authority for any children's home to ensure that certain precautions are taken against the risk of fire and to contain and reduce the risk to the children in the case of an outbreak of fire.

Amendment to the Disqualification for Caring for Children Regulations 1991

Amending Regulation: Regulation 5(2) of the Children (Protection from Offenders) (Miscellaneous Amendments) Regulations 1997

This amends the principal regulations by adding to the list of convictions which disqualify a person from fostering a child privately, being registered as a child minder or being involved in certain other activities involving children, a conviction for or caution in respect of any of the offences which would prevent such a person from being considered suitable to adopt or foster a child.

Amendment to the Child Minding and Day Care (Registration and Inspection Fees) Regulations 1991

Amending Regulation: Regulation 2(2) of the Child Minding and Day Care (Registration and Inspection Fees) (Amendment) Regulations 1996

This increases the registration fees for providers of full day care on non-domestic premises from £100 to £110 and for providers of sessional day care and child minders from £10 to £12.50.

Amending Regulation: Regulation 2(3) of the Child Minding and Day Care (Registration and Inspection Fees) (Amendment) Regulations 1996

This increases annual inspection fees.

Amendment to the Children Act 1989

Amending Regulation: Regulation 2 Children Act 1989 (Amendment) (Children Services Planning) Order 1996

This amends Schedule 2 of the Children Act 1989 so that after paragraph 1 there is inserted paragraph 1A "Children's services plans". This requires local authorities to prepare and publish plans for the provision of children's services in their area and keep those plans under review. In preparing or updating their plans local authorities are required to consult health and education authorities, certain voluntary organisations, police, probation services and other relevant bodies. The Secretary of State may require the local authority to submit these plans to him at any time.

Amendment to the Secure Accommodation Regulations 1991

Amending Regulation: Regulation 3 of the Children (Homes and Secure Accommodation) (Miscellaneous Amendments) Regulations 1996

This amends regulation 2 of the principal regulations to extend the requirements relating to the keeping of records in relation to children in secure accommodation to apply to other persons or organisations managing such accommodation.

Amending Regulation: Regulation 6 of the Children (Secure Accommodation) Amendments Regulations 1995

This revokes regulation 18 of the principal Regulations that prohibited the use of accommodation for the purpose of restricting the liberty of children in voluntary homes and registered children's homes.

Amending Regulation: Regulation 2,3,4 and 5 of the Children (Secure Accommodation) Amendments Regulations 1995

This makes amendments to regulations 2,3,4,9,14,15,16, 17 of the principal regulations. These amendments are made in connection with the extension of provision of secure accommodation enacted in section 19 of the Criminal Justice and Public Order 1994 which amended Schedules 5 and 6 of the Children Act 1989 and removed the power to prohibit the use of certain accommodation as secure accommodation. The principal regulations are thereby amended to apply the provisions of those Regulations which govern secure accommodation in community homes to secure accommodation in voluntary homes and registered children's homes.

Amendment to the Arrangement for Placement of Children Regulations 1991

Amending Regulation: Regulation 3 of the Children (short-term placements) (Miscellaneous Amendments) Regulations 1995

This substitutes a new regulation 13(1) into the principal regulations which modifies the total length of time for which a series of short term placements may last and still be regarded as one placement.

Amendment to the Placement of Children with Parents etc Regulations 1991

Amending Regulation: Regulation 4 of the Children (short-term placements) (Miscellaneous Amendments) Regulations 1995

This substitutes new sub-paragraphs (1) and (3) into regulation 13 of the principal regulations. This modifies the total length of time for which a series of short-term placements may last and still be regarded as one placement for the purposes of certain requirements and also modifies the requirements for visits to supervise a series of short term placements.

Amendment to the Review of Children's Cases Regulations 1991

Amending Regulation: Regulation 5 of the Children (short-term placements) (Miscellaneous Amendments) Regulations 1995

This substitutes a new regulation 11 into the principal regulations. This modifies the total length of time for which a series of short-term placements may last and still be regarded as one placement. It also makes special provision for review of cases where there is a series of short-term placement.

Amendment to the Parental Responsibility Agreement Regulations 1991

Amending Regulations: the Parental Responsibility Agreement (Amendment) Regulations 1994

These amend the principal regulations by prescribing a new form for the recording of an agreement between the parents of a child that the father is to have parental responsibility for the child within the meaning of section 3 of the Children Act 1989. It changes the layout and content of the form to make it easier to understand and complete.

Amendment to the Children (Allocation of Proceedings) Order 1991

Amending Regulations: the Children (Allocation of Proceedings) (Amendment) Order 1998

This amends article 6(2) of the original order which deals with the allocation and transfer between courts of family proceedings so as to provide for the transfer of child safety orders (the proceedings for which are now designated as family proceedings under the Children Act 1989) between magistrates courts.

Amending Regulations: Articles 2 & 3 of the Children (Allocation of Proceedings) (Amendment) Order 1997

Article 2 extends the power of county courts to review the refusal by a magistrate's court to the transfer of proceedings to a county court.

Article 3 extends the power to provide for cases to be transferred from county courts to magistrates courts.

Amending Regulation: Regulation 3 of the Children (Allocation of Proceedings) (Amendment) Order 1994

This inserts words which have the effect of extending the original order to proceedings under Section 30 of the Human Fertilisation and Embryology Act 1990 (parental orders in favour of gamete donors). The effect of the order is to require such proceedings to be commenced in a magistrates court and to provide for them to be transferred to other courts in certain circumstances.

Amendment to the Guardians Ad Litem and Reporting Officers (Panels) Regulations 1991.

Amending Regulation: Regulation 2 of the Guardians Ad Litem and Reporting Officers (Panels) (Amendment) Regulations 1997.

This makes several minor changes but importantly it makes the following amendments:

Regulation 2(5) inserts a new regulation 4A into the principal regulations entitled "Non re-appointment to panel". This provides that where a local authority proposed not to reappoint a guardian ad litem or reporting officer to its panel at the end of their existing appointment, they are to be given notice of the reasons for that proposal and the opportunity to make representations. The membership of persons who are not re-appointed may be extended to enable them to finish work on their current case load.

Regulation 2(6) amends regulation 5 of the principal regulations by inserting new paragraphs (6) and (7). These allow local authorities to establish joint complaints boards to consider termination of the panel membership of a guardian ad litem or reporting officer who is a member of each of the authorities panels, if the authorities' reasons for proposing to terminate membership are similar or related.

Regulation 2(7) amends regulation 6 of the principal regulations by inserting a new paragraph (5). This applies where a guardian ad litem or reporting officer is a member of more than one panel and related complaints about him are made to more than one local authority. The authorities may in those circumstances agree to investigate the complaints jointly.

Regulation 2(8) inserts a new regulation 6A into the principal regulations. This provides that the courts are to be informed about serious complaints directed towards panel members. The local authority may decide that the panel member concerned should not be made available for appointment in new cases until the complaint has been investigated.

Regulation 2(9) amends regulation 8 (panel committee functions) of the principal regulations by substituting a new sub-paragraph (d). This modifies the functions of committee panel to enable the committee to advise on the handling of complaints about a panel member or the administration of the panel.

Regulation 2(10) amends regulation 9(2) of the principal regulations. This amendment clarifies that local authorities may reimburse all guardians for expenses incurred in connection with their work, whether they are employed by the authority or self employed.

Regulation 2(11) amends the principal regulations by inserting a new regulation 13 entitled "contracting out of functions in relation to the provision of panels of guardians ad litem and reporting officers. This makes a consequential amendment to regulation 5(7) and Schedule 1 of the principal regulations where local authority functions under those regulations are contracted out to another person.

Regulations 2(12) and 2(13) amend Schedules 1 and 2 of the principal regulations so that any justices' clerk or deputy to a justices' clerk may sit on a complaints board.

Printed in the UK for The Stationery Office Limited on behalf of the
Controller of Her Majesty's Stationery Office
Dd 5067426, 1/00, 77240, Job No TJ 000213